Writing against God

Language as Message in the Literature of Flannery O'Connor

Writing against God

Language as Message in the Literature of Flannery O'Connor

Joanne Halleran McMullen

MERCER UNIVERSITY PRESS
Macon, Georgia · 1996

ISBN 0-86654-488-3

Writing against God:
Language as Message in the Literature of Flannery O'Connor
by Joanne Halleran McMullen

Mercer University Press, Macon, Georgia 31210-3960 USA

Printed in the United States of America.

The paper used in this publication meets the minimum requirements of American National Standard for Information Sciences—Permanence of Paper for Printed Library Materials, ANSI Z39.48-1984.

Library of Congress Cataloging-in-Publication Data

McMullen, Joanne Halleran.
Writing against God: language as message in the literature of Flannery O'Connor / Joanne Halleran McMullen.
viii + 152 pp. 6x9"
Includes bibliographic references and index.
ISBN 0-86554-488-3 (alk. paper)
1. O'Connor, Flannery—Criticism and interpretation. 2. Authors and readers—Southern States—History—20th century. 3. Women and literature—Southern States—History—20th century. 4. Christian fiction, American—History and criticism. 5. Christianity and literature—Southern States. 6. Reader-response criticism. 7. God in literature. I. Title.
PS3565.C57Z784 1996
813'.54—dc20 96-11880

Contents

Abbreviations

The abbreviations of O'Connor's works commonly cited in the text refer to the following editions:

Collected *Flannery O'Connor: Collected Works*. Edited by Sally Fitzgerald. New York: Library of America, 1988.

CS *The Complete Stories*. Introduced by Robert Giroux. New York: Farrar, Straus, and Giroux, 1986.

ERMC *Everything That Rises Must Converge*. Introduced by Robert Fitzgerald. New York: Farrar, Straus, and Giroux, 1965.

HB *The Habit of Being: Letters of Flannery O'Connor*. Edited by Sally Fitzgerald. New York: Farrar, Straus, and Giroux, 1979.

MM *Mystery and Manners*: *Occasional Prose*. Edited by Sally and Robert Fitzgerald. New York: Farrar, Straus, and Giroux, 1969.

For Bob, Rob, and Bridget

Introduction

Flannery O'Connor repeatedly categorized herself as a Catholic writer. She felt her stories conveyed an unquestioning Catholic outlook on the Fall, the Incarnation, and finally the Redemption. Disturbed by what she considered the misreading of her stories, she has interpreted her works in various letters and talks as not only extolling Christian virtue, but more specifically Catholic virtue. Her declarations have attracted critics who adamantly agree that her work embodies Catholic doctrine as well as those who firmly posit the opposite. While it is possible to recognize her fervor for Catholic doctrine in her letters and speeches and, therefore, postulate that in all likelihood she believed her writing consistent with Catholic dogma, not all who come to her fictional works can easily perceive this relationship. Readers throughout the years have often "misread" her intentions or disagreed with O'Connor's interpretations of her own fictional product. Style, symbolism, image, metaphor, structure, and theme often belie O'Connor's insistence of her Catholic message to many readers unacquainted with her fervent explications in lectures and letters.

Marshall Bruce Gentry in *Flannery O'Connor's Religion of the Grotesque* outlines the extreme variance in O'Connor's critical assessment. He states that there are "four critical schools" of O'Connor criticism ranging from the degree (if any) of religious design in her fiction to a belief that her "artistry is demonic."[1] Gentry sums up these critical schools with a representative proponent of each, thus:

1. Carol Shloss "denies the realization of theological intent";

2. Carter Martin and Kathleen Feeley "consider O'Connor's outlook to be orthodoxly Catholic";

3. Martha Stephens and Miles Orvell regard O'Connor's religious stance as "overly harsh";

4. Josephine Hendin, John Hawkes, and Claire Katz Kahane see the "demonic" in O'Connor's work.[2]

---

[1]Marshall Bruce Gentry, *Flannery O'Connor's Religion of the Grotesque* (Jackson: University Press of Mississippi, 1986) 3.

[2]Ibid.

While it is possible to understand how each of these schools has its supporters, I suggest that a fifth school of criticism, a school that emphasizes the deliberate mystery O'Connor has so cleverly and abstrusely concealed throughout her fiction with her careful language choices, would more accurately assess O'Connor's literary contributions. When O'Connor's work is examined linguistically and the response of readers unschooled in O'Connor criticism is taken into account, it is clearly possible for the critic to shed previously held biases and uncover startling evidence that ultimately makes clear how intentionally enigmatic O'Connor's fictional message truly is, and thus how such widely varying and even antithetically differing critical views can be possible.

O'Connor would, of course, be delighted to be considered a critical mystery and would be amused to think of her work as continuing to engender controversy. Yet her use of mystery was a carefully conscious effort to use language that would create within her fictional microcosm the embodiment of the Divine Mystery elusively at work in a world of sin and evil. She expressly set out to retell the mystery of the Incarnation and enfolded it skillfully within her fiction. When we as readers allow ourselves to come anew to O'Connor's fiction, we discover the amazingly intricate complexities she has so subtly woven into her work. We can then fully appreciate that dissention among her critics emanates from O'Connor's precise linguistic choices and is not only possible but rather is inescapable.

In *Pragmatic Aspects of English Text Structure* Larry Bert Jones states, "Human communication depends on assumption making."[3] He illustrates this assertion by stating that "an author's assumptions about his reader's knowledge have an especially strong impact on the grammatical and semantic shape of a text."[4] He cites rhetoricians Young, Becker, and Pike's view: "It is important to remember that the writer addresses his discourse not to the reader as he 'really is' but to the image of the reader that he has developed in his own mind."[5] Flannery O'Connor, as any writer, therefore, was affected by her assumptions of her audience. In her own mind she perceived her reading public not as non-believers but as unbelievers hostile to what she called Christian mystery. On 2 August

[3]Larry Bert Jones, *Pragmatic Aspects of English Text Structure* (Dallas: Summer Institute of Linguistics and the University of Texas at Arlington, 1983) 1.

[4]Ibid., 3.

[5]Ibid., as quoted in.

1955, she wrote to "A": "My audience are the people who think God is dead. At least these are the people I am conscious of writing for" (*Collected* 943). Because O'Connor was fiercely convinced of the religious shortcomings of her reading public, she considered it her duty as a Catholic writer to reach this audience controlled by unbelief. On this subject she wrote in the essay "The Fiction Writer & His Country":

> When you can assume that your audience holds the same beliefs you do, you can relax a little and use more normal means of talking to it; when you have to assume that it does not, then you have to make your vision apparent by shock—to the hard of hearing you shout, and for the almost-blind you draw large and startling figures. (*MM* 34)

Given her views of her audience, and as part of her dogmatic Christian intent, O'Connor deliberately chose to stun her readers with her bizarre characters, plots, and themes to awaken them to God's message, and to do so in a style that drew broad figures for a blind audience. Her reading public, however, comes to her fiction with assumptions about Southern gothic humor, religious fundamentalism, and Catholicism that condition their readings. For as Louise Rosenblatt states:

> The reader, too, is creative. The text may produce that moment of balanced perception, a complete esthetic experience. But it will not be the result of passivity on the reader's part; the literary experience must be phrased as a *transaction* between the reader and the text. Moreover, as in the creative activity of the artist, there will be selective factors molding the reader's response. He comes to the book from life.[6]

Most readers of Flannery O'Connor's fiction come away from her works not able to merge their Christian beliefs with the experience of O'Connor's stories. In his essay "The Idea of a Psychoanalytic Literary Criticism," while not totally advocating theories such as Rosenblatt's, Peter Brooks does agree that reader-response criticism "has usefully shown us that the reader necessarily collaborates and competes in the creation of

---

[6]Louise M. Rosenblatt, *Literature as Exploration* (New York: Noble and Noble, Publishers, Inc., 1976) 34-35.

textual meaning."[7] Recognizing that this competitive process can often result in conflicts, Walker Gibson writes:

> The fact is that every time we open the pages of another piece of writing, we are embarked on a new adventure in which we become a new person—a person as controlled and definable and as remote from the chaotic self of daily life as the lover in the sonnet. Subject to the degree of our literary sensibility, we are recreated by the language. We assume, for the sake of the experience, that set of attitudes and qualities which the language asks us to assume, and, if we cannot assume them, we throw the book away.[8]

Readers enthralled by O'Connor's fictional artistry do not "throw the book away" when they cannot assume her intended Catholic message. Instead, they construct creative "misreadings" until they become "educated" by her own declarations or those of her critics.

Because Flannery O'Connor brought to her fiction her own version of Catholicism in all of its idiosyncrasy, many of her readers, both Christian and non-Christian, Catholic and non-Catholic, have had difficulties in perceiving her works as supportive of Church doctrines. There have additionally been features of O'Connor's style that have led readers away from receiving her professed Catholic message. In a 1961 article in the Catholic journal *Renascence*, Robert Bowen, an early critic of O'Connor's second novel, questions O'Connor's faithfulness to the dogmas of her Catholic upbringing. He writes:

> After even a casual perusal of *The Violent Bear It Away*, the only reason one might refer to Flannery O'Connor as a "Catholic" author is a personal one. Since this novel has been widely spoken of as "Catholic," it seems imperative that one point out that like so much current negative writing, this book is not Catholic at all in any doctrinal sense. Neither its content nor its significance is Catholic. Beyond not being Catholic, the novel is distinctly anti-Catholic in being a thorough, point-

[7]Peter Brooks, "The Idea of a Psychoanalytic Literary Criticism," in *Discourse in Psychoanalysis and Literature*, ed. Shlomith Rimmon-Kenan. (London: Methuen & Co. Ltd., 1987) 11.

[8]Walker Gibson, "Authors, Speakers, Readers, and Mock Readers," in *Reader-Response Criticism: From Formalism to Post-Structuralism*, ed. Tompkins, 1.

> by-point dramatic argument against Free Will, Redemption, and Divine Justice, among other aspects of Catholic thought.[9]

When we consider that "the use of one type of grammatical construction in a text instead of other grammatically appropriate constructions at that point is assumed not to be a matter of mere random variation but one of meaningful (though not necessarily conscious) choice," it becomes necessary to scrutinize O'Connor's textual choices carefully.[10]

Chapter 1 ("Stylistic Techniques of Annihilation") explores some of the reasons the reader's response to O'Connor must be explicitly coached if reader interpretations are to match O'Connor's explications. This chapter focuses on a linguistic analysis of O'Connor's literary style, a style that makes use of mainly simple sentences, an overwhelming preponderance of pronouns, the substitution of bodily parts for a character, a heavy reliance on passive voice and passive participial adjectives, verb choices forcing inaction, and naming techniques that obscure or minimize personal worth.

Chapter 2 ("Symbolic Barriers to Salvation") addresses the problems O'Connor's symbols pose for readers. O'Connor imbues familiar objects with symbolic power. Hats, sunlight, eyes, eyeglasses, colors, wood, animals, and machinery all take on symbolic meaning in her fiction. In this chapter, the lack of symbolic consistency from story to story as well as within stories confound the perceptions of her readers suddenly unable to reconcile the treatment of character and symbol with the redemptive fates of her tormented souls.

Chapter 3 ("Images Versus Religious Intent in O'Connor's Fiction") centers on imagery that compliments O'Connor's symbols in their inconsistency of use and in their idiosyncrasy. This chapter examines O'Connor's immense writing talent which effortlessly disguises her message within images seemingly familiar. Upon scrutiny, however, these images of the Georgia landscape, familial relationships, the Christ figure, inanimate objects, death, and Christian humanism take on unexpected meanings and on close inspection appear not to support her stated Catholic views.

---

[9]Robert O. Bowen, "Hope vs. Despair in the New Gothic Novel," in *Renascence: A Critical Journal of Letters* 13/3 (Spring 1961): 150. A review of *The Violent Bear It Away*.

[10]Jones, *Pragmatic Aspects of English Text Structure*, 5.

Chapter 4 ("Catholic Themes in the Works of O'Connor") reviews several predominate themes in O'Connor's works and argues against their adherence to the Catholicism of her day. The Catholic concept of a sacramental marriage, the Church's stance on birth control, and the sanctity of the family are viewed against O'Connor's private comments.

Chapter 5 ("The Grammar of Negation") dissects O'Connor's language to reveal the overwhelming negation present in her fictional world. Negative words, negative verbs, anagrams, the concept of suffering, mysterious concealments, and directional metaphors all work in O'Connor's fiction to negate the action of grace presumably available to her characters.

Chapter 6 ("The Verbal Structure of Infinity") acquaints readers with O'Connor's storytelling techniques as they relate to time references in her fiction. O'Connor's ability to incorporate eternal time within her fiction through circular structuring emphases her artistic control. She determines the destiny of her tortured beings through repetition, intransitivity, the use of compound verbs and compound sentence constructions, and time references as indicated by adverbials and verb tense choices. As this chapter demonstrates, circular patterning acts as an inclusion or exclusion device for her characters as they strive for grace.

Frederick Crews writes that O'Connor's style was shaped by the New Criticism university workshop approach and that

> Even the most impressive and original of her stories adhere to the classroom formula of her day: show, don't tell; keep the narrative voice distinct from those of your characters; cultivate understatement; develop a central image or symbol to convey your theme "objectively"; and point everything toward one neatly sprung ironic reversal.[11]

The approach to writing that O'Connor learned at the Iowa workshop is in opposition to the polemical demands of making the work embody Catholic doctrine. Despite her desire to make the stories serve religious ends, the "show" the characters act out, the language they use, and the internal structure of their fictional world often seem to tell a very

[11]Frederick Crews, "The Power of Flannery O'Connor," *The New York Review of Books* 37/7 (26 April 1990): 49.

different story. Readers are confronted with an authorial intent in conflict with a dramatic enactment, and for many, the drama of the characters overwhelms the clarity of the author's stated purposes.

In a letter to "A" dated 20 July 1955, O'Connor discussed the ideas that inform her writing:

> I write the way I do because (not though) I am a Catholic. . . . However, I am a Catholic peculiarly possessed of the modern consciousness. . . . To possess this *within* the Church is to bear a burden, the necessary burden for the conscious Catholic. It's to feel the contemporary situation at the ultimate level. I think that the Church is the only thing that is going to make the terrible world we are coming to endurable; the only thing that makes the Church endurable is that it is somehow the body of Christ and that on this we are fed. (*Collected* 942)

For O'Connor, however, very often the "body of Christ" is embodied in vicious figures such as The Misfit in "A Good Man Is Hard to Find," a character who may easily raise questions as to how her Church can make the terrible endurable if grace comes at the end of his gun. In *Mystery and Manners* O'Connor does acknowledge that her writings give emphasis to the terrible:

> when I look at stories I have written I find that they are, for the most part, about people who are poor, who are afflicted in both mind and body, who have little—or at best a distorted—sense of spiritual purpose, and whose actions do not apparently give the reader a great assurance of the joy of life. (*MM* 32)

The dilemma persists, therefore, for readers to see the endurable in her spiritually distorted souls.

O'Connor's concern with her audience's perception of her as a writer dominates her private correspondence:

> I am mighty tired of reading reviews that call "A Good Man" brutal and sarcastic. The stories are hard but they are hard because there is nothing harder or less sentimental than Christian realism. I believe that there are many rough beasts now slouching toward Bethlehem to be born and that I have reported the progress of a few of them, and when I see these stories described as horror stories I am always amused because the reviewer always has hold of the wrong horror. (*Collected* 942)

In November 1955, during the early years of her writing, O'Connor commented in a letter to John Lynch that she received little notice by Catholic critics. She considered this ironic because as she reported in a statement that echoed her comments to "A" made earlier in the same year: "I write the way I do because and only because I am a Catholic. I feel that if I were not a Catholic, I would have no reason to write, no reason to see, no reason ever to feel horrified or even to enjoy anything" (*HB* 114). She ended her letter to Lynch with her conviction that she had been "formed by the Church." Once again in a 1955 letter to "A," O'Connor reaffirmed her connection with the Catholic Church when she wrote that for her "the ultimate reality is the Incarnation, the present reality is the Incarnation, the whole reality is the Incarnation" (*Collected* 943).

Notwithstanding her repeated insistence that "the whole reality is the Incarnation," the texts of the stories establish a narrative logic that often works against thematic intent. By examining the language and style O'Connor uses to impart ideas she considers Catholic in her two novels and several of her major short stories, we shall come to a better understanding of how her audience is forced to focus on "the wrong horror" in her works despite her impassioned exclamations. Because of her language choices, readers are often compelled into a non-Catholic, and yes, sometimes even an anti-Catholic reading of her fiction. In part because her writings are carefully crafted adhering in many ways to a formula emphasizing "show, don't tell," the characters and actions shown argue their own point, often turning in an ironic reversal against the author.

1.
Stylistic Techniques of Annihilation

Approaching Flannery O'Connor's fiction with an awareness that she possessed a zealous desire to enlighten a godless world through the medium of her fictional message enables us to explain O'Connor's simple, yet never simplistic, writing style. O'Connor's sentence constructions demonstrate that she was undeniably aware that she must be accessible to her reading public. In *Mystery and Manners* she states:

> I wouldn't want to suggest that the Georgia writer has the unanimous, collective ear of his community, but only that his true audience, the audience he checks himself by, is at home. (*MM* 54)

Stylistically, for instance, most of her short stories begin with simple subject-verb constructions in which the main character as subject performs some action. The following story titles from *The Complete Stories* with abbreviated first sentences are illustrative of O'Connor's formulaic patterning:

> From "The Geranium":
> Old Dudley folded into the chair. . .
>
> From "Wildcat":
> Old Gabriel shuffled across the room . . .
>
> From "The Crop":
> Miss Willerton always crumbed the table.
>
> From "The Peeler":
> Hazel Motes walked along downtown . . .
>
> From "A Stroke of Good Fortune":
> Ruby came in the front door . . .
>
> From "The Lame Shall Enter First":
> Sheppard sat on a stool . . .
>
> From "Judgement Day":
> Tanner was conserving all his strength . . .
> (*CS* 3; 26; 33; 63; 95; 445; 531)

In fact, O'Connor's sentence structure throughout her fiction often follows the same predictable pattern of beginning with subject-verb sentence constructions with simple declarative sentences most prevalent. While O'Connor does employ complex sentences in her fiction, simple sentences by far predominate. The opening paragraph from "The Lame Shall Enter First" serves as an example:

> Sheppard sat on a stool at the bar that divided the kitchen in half, eating his cereal out of the individual pasteboard box it came in. He ate mechanically, his eyes on the child, who was wandering from cabinet to cabinet in the panelled kitchen, collecting the ingredients for his breakfast. He was a stocky blond boy of ten. Sheppard kept his intense blue eyes fixed on him. The boy's future was written in his face. He would be a banker. No, worse. He would operate a small loan company. All he wanted for the child was that he be good and unselfish and neither seemed likely. Sheppard was a young man whose hair was already white. It stood up like a narrow brush halo over his pink sensitive face. (*CS* 445)

This beginning paragraph, while it does have four complex sentences, is composed primarily of simple sentences, six in all, and in all but one case every sentence begins with the subject directly followed by the verb. The next paragraph follows a similar pattern. Of a total of five sentences, three are simple declarative, and all begin with the subject followed directly by the verb.

While this apparent declarative simplicity does permit readability and, therefore, a kind of accessibility because of its almost journalistic narrative style, it also sets up a pattern of realistic expectations on the part of O'Connor's audience that trustingly expects that the story's events and characters will act out their dynamic in this recognizably concrete social world. When the "ironic reversals" take us out of this familiar environment to a vision of heaven or a moment of mysterious revelation, the reader may instead "complete" the story by relying on expectations that O'Connor's style has seemingly set up. Instead of suddenly seeing the mystery revealed, however, the reader transposes the images intended to reveal the religious presence into images with more mundane associations. Thus, the good man *is* hard to find because language and events in the realistic narrative have given us a brutal murder whose meaning we look for in humanistic terms instead of O'Connor's hint of Grace that has its efficacy in a world beyond the constructed one in the story.

In *Prose Style and Critical Reading*, Robert Cluett details linguistic features that categorize an author's literary style. The style that seems to approximate O'Connor's most closely is the nominal rather than verbal style. While Cluett's study was concerned with the class of words that accompany a nominal or verbal style, my interest has been in determining whether O'Connor's style is mainly nominal or verbal. Taking just the first paragraph of several of O'Connor's short stories as examples, I have used a simple count of nouns versus verbs. To the noun count I added relative pronouns, and pronouns; for the verb count I included verbals (infinitives and participles) and main verbs, although all parts of the main verb, should the tense require multiple parts, were counted as one. The stories surveyed span the length of O'Connor's writing career; they are: "The Geranium," "Judgement Day," "A Temple of the Holy Ghost," "A View of the Woods," and "A Late Encounter with the Enemy" as they appear in *The Complete Stories*. In just the first paragraphs of all of these stories, nouns/pronouns outnumber verbs/verbals by the following ratios: 1.88 to 1 ("The Geranium"), 1.95 to 1 ("Judgement Day"), 2.14 to 1 ("A Temple of the Holy Ghost"), 2.35 to 1 ("A View of the Woods") and 2.39 to 1 ("A Late Encounter with the Enemy"). Using just this brief sampling, it is apparent that O'Connor's style falls into the nominal rather than verbal category.

One might think that use of a nominal style would indicate concern for people. However, despite the fact that O'Connor's prose style employs a high density of nouns, the nouns she uses are not, for the most part, for character reference. Instead, O'Connor has a penchant for referring to her characters pronominally. As an example, on the first page of the story "Greenleaf," O'Connor uses nineteen pronouns in either the subject or object positions in the first four paragraphs. Mrs. May, the main character, does appear in the opening sentence of the story; however, she does not appear in the form of a noun or a pronoun reference, but rather in the possessive form as the owner of the "bedroom window" (*CS* 311). Also on this first page, Mrs. May's voice, again, not Mrs. May the person, achieves status. In fact, O'Connor further distances the reader's access to Mrs. May the person, by using the indefinite article and a non-specific possessive reference to her voice. The sentence reads:

> For almost a minute there was no sound from inside, then as he raised his crowned head again, a woman's voice, guttural as if addressed to a

dog, said, "Get away from here, Sir!" and in a second muttered, "Some nigger's scrub bull." (*CS* 311)

Mrs. May, the individual to whom O'Connor will teach the ultimate lesson, is finally mentioned once nominally but not until the third paragraph of the story. From this point onward, however, Mrs. May again only appears as a pronoun reference until the end of page 4. Two operants here affect the reader's response: the use of bodily parts to complete an action, and the preponderance of the third-person pronoun.

Geoffrey Leech and Michael Short indicate that the "use of a bodily part instead of a person as an actor in a clause is a fairly common device for suggesting that the part of the body involved acts of its own accord."[1] Chris Kennedy concurs that distancing results when "Parts of the body take on the role of actor."[2] O'Connor frequently employs this linguistic technique as a replacement for character actions as the following sentences and/or partial sentences from *The Complete Stories of Flannery O'Connor* indicate:

From "The Displaced Person":
Mrs. Shortley's mouth had drawn acidly to one side.
The patched face did not say. (*CS* 198; 223)

From "Good Country People":
The boy's astonished eyes looked blankly through the ends of her hair.
The boy's mouth was set angrily. (*CS* 288; 290)

From "The Lame Shall Enter First":
Sheppard's mouth stretched in disgust.
Johnson's sad thin hand rooted in garbage cans for food . . .
Johnson's mouth twisted slightly.
The child's pale eyes hardened in disbelief.
Johnson's finger moved under the lines they were reading.
(*CS* 446; 449; 451; 461; 475)

---

[1]Geoffrey N. Leech and Michael H. Short, *Style in Fiction: A Linguistic Introduction to English Fictional Prose* (London: Longman, 1981) 190.

[2]Chris Kennedy, "Systemic Grammar and its Use in Literary Analysis," in *Language and Literature: An Introductory Reader in Stylistics*, ed. Ronald Carter, 88.

In these sentences disconnected body parts seemingly act on their own behalf, severing themselves from their owners. O'Connor's insistence on character anonymity through this distancing technique banishes her fictional characters to personal insignificance and steer the reader away from viewing them as whole people who actively take part in the completion of God's scheme.

In both short stories and novels O'Connor's unrelenting reliance on the third-person pronoun becomes another method that "distances the author and the reader from the character it denotes."[3] Pronoun referents in *The Violent Bear It Away*, in addition to creating a barrier toward character association, bewilder the reader. O'Connor's obfuscations in this novel begin with muddled character relationships that obscure character identification from even a diligent reader. Old Tarwater is both an uncle and a great-uncle in the story, although his relationship is primarily considered to be "uncle" throughout. Young Tarwater is a nephew and great-nephew, although his "nephew" status dominates. Additionally, there is the character Rayber, son of Rayber, who himself is either uncle or nephew to the two Tarwaters.

As if this genealogical imbroglio were not cloudy enough, O'Connor's indiscriminate use of the pronoun "he," which refers to all of these male characters in settings that are vague at best, causes the reader to become lost in a tangle of pronominal non-referents. In discussing Young Tarwater's visit to the lawyer's office with Old Tarwater, O'Connor mentions that "Tarwater had sat at the lawyer's twelfth-story window and looked down into the pit of the street while his uncle transacted the business" (*Collected* 346). After some lengthy major digressions which take the reader away from Tarwater's presence at the office window, O'Connor again returns to this scene. However, the office window scenario is preceded by Young Tarwater talking to Old Tarwater about missions of prophecy. The following dialogue ensues:

> The boy paled slightly and his gaze shifted. "I ain't been called *yet*," he muttered. "It's you that's been called."
>
> "And I know what times I'm called and what times I ain't," his uncle said and turned and paid him no more attention.
>
> At the lawyer's window, he knelt down and let his face hang out upsidedown over the floating speckled street moving like a river of tin

[3]Leech and Short, *Style in Fiction*, 18.

> below and watched the glints on it from the sun which drifted pale in a pale sky, too far away to ignite anything. (*Collected* 347)

Ordinarily, in the interest of clarity, the person mentioned as the subject immediately preceding a pronoun reference would be the person referred to by the pronoun. As this excerpt shows, however, O'Connor follows a direct reference to the uncle Tarwater with a new sentence in which the "he" refers not to the antecedent uncle, but to the nephew who appears only pronominally and in a subordinate position in the sentence before. Only from our recollection of the explicit information provided much earlier on the preceding page, or from our implicit knowledge that hanging upsidedown from a window is inherently childlike behavior, can we come to the conclusion that the "he" who is hanging out of the lawyer's window, is, in fact, Young Tarwater. O'Connor dismisses the possibility of substituting a nominal referent in place of this pronominal construction, a referent that would both clarify and stress the importance of who speaks or acts. One might try to explain this away by insisting that O'Connor was perhaps attempting to create an "Everyman" to whom her impious audience could relate, but a closer look at O'Connor's handling of personal pronouns calls this interpretation into question.

In *The Violent Bear It Away*, in one of his flashbacks, Rayber remembers his wife's encounter with Young Tarwater as the baby they would attempt to rescue. O'Connor, as third-person narrator, describes Rayber's wife's impressions:

> It was not simply that the child was dirty, thin, and grey; it was that its expression had no more changed when the gun went off than the old man's had. This had affected her deeply. (*Collected* 441)

O'Connor makes a subtle shift in her narration to free indirect style which functions "to combine and superimpose the words (voice and linguistic forms) of the narrator and his characters."[4] By overlaying her thoughts as narrator onto the thoughts of her character, the welfare woman, O'Connor twice reinforces the concept of the baby Tarwater as a non-person:

---

[4]Pierre Guiraud, "Modern Linguistics Looks at Rhetoric: Free Indirect Style," in *Patterns of Literary Style*, ed. Joseph Strelka, 86.

> If there had not been something repellent in its face, she said, her maternal instinct would have made her rush forward and snatch it (*Collected* 442).

Five more times either O'Connor as omniscient narrator, or Rayber's wife in free indirect style, refers to the child directly with the pronoun "it," which is generally reserved, when used for people, to refer to unborn children or babies for whom the sex is unknown. Rayber's wife, however, knows Young Tarwater's sex, as does O'Connor as author-creator. O'Connor refers to this male child repeatedly in this passage by a pronoun used in the main for animals or inanimate objects. Pronouns here do not seem to be used with ambiguity to create an "Everyman/ Everywoman." The reader, instead, is confronted on a subliminal level with a human child linguistically minified through O'Connor's use of the neutral pronoun "it." Strangely this non-person referent becomes juxtaposed in this passage with the concept "maternal instinct." Not only does it seem incongruous to unite a baby seen so impersonally as to be considered an "it" with the idea of "mother," but it is inconsistent to link this welfare woman with such a notion. She certainly is not the loving, nurturing figure one would customarily associate with motherhood. The woman wants not to cradle or hold this child; she wants to "snatch it."

Rayber's wife is repulsed by the child she views as an "it," whose "look had frozen her." And O'Connor even writes that this woman "could not have lived with such a face, she would have been bound to destroy the arrogant look on it" (*Collected* 442). The child has become linguistically annihilated by the pronoun O'Connor uses to refer to him. And because O'Connor surrounds the child with harsh, disapproving, even violent language in his connection to the welfare woman, the reader is left with little doubt that should Rayber's wife have the opportunity she would literally annihilate this human baby. O'Connor's language concentrates on obliterating the personal worth of her fictional creations and then persecutes these beings made invisible with intense animosity. Such techniques work toward destroying the personal worth of her characters stylistically generating misunderstandings for those readers searching for a link to the human caring expected in Christianity in general and Catholicism in particular.

O'Connor's fascination with pronouns, which pervade her fiction, can also be seen in her story endings. Her story endings, like her story beginnings, continue this impersonal stylistic technique and set up further tensions between her stated intentions and the reader's response. In the final sentences of all of her stories, with the exceptions of "A Good Man Is Hard to Find," "The Artificial Nigger," "Good Country People," and "Parker's Back," O'Connor avoids proper names and uses only pronouns. In fact, throughout her entire canon, and not just in her story introductions and conclusions, O'Connor indicates her indifference toward her characters as beings in possession of unique personalities through pronoun use and unclear referents. This linguistic effacing of characters becomes O'Connor's rhetorical imprint as her language choices tend toward the annihilation of the individual. Readers who come to her stories associating modern Catholicism with a concern for humanity encounter, instead, a medieval theological emphasis on the redemption of souls for the glory of God.

In addition to pronoun references and ambiguity, O'Connor continually deemphasizes the importance of individuals through naming techniques and an avoidance of names altogether. In "Good Country People," Joy herself changes the name her mother (and O'Connor) gave her. She, and O'Connor, decide on "Hulga" because as O'Connor writes:

> She had a vision of the name working like the ugly sweating Vulcan who stayed in the furnace and to whom, presumably, the goddess had to come when called. She saw it as the name of her highest creative act. One of her major triumphs was that her mother had not been able to turn her dust into Joy, but the greater one was that she had been able to turn it herself into Hulga. (*CS* 275)

As important as the creation of this name seems to be to both O'Connor and Joy, after Joy-Hulga decides to meet and seduce the Bible salesman, the name "Hulga" is only used twice. O'Connor has the Bible salesman refer to her by name when he first meets her for their "picnic." To her question of why he brought his Bibles he answers, "You can never tell when you'll need the word of God, Hulga" (*CS* 285). And finally, at the end of the story when he has violated her spiritually, O'Connor has him say:

> "And I'll tell you another thing, Hulga," he said, using the name as if he didn't think much of it, "you ain't so smart. I been believing in nothing ever since I was born!". . . (*CS* 291)

O'Connor's uses of "Hulga" at the beginning and end of this episode function as a framing device within which she establishes her main character's spiritual fate. She ironically has the Bible salesman signal that Hulga, the individual, might need the word of God, but for six pages Hulga's individuality is ignored. Not until she has been absolutely annihilated and left spiritually, emotionally, and physically devastated to consider her fate does O'Connor give her back her name. But this only for a moment, for O'Connor leaves Hulga with the sentence: "the girl was left, sitting on the straw in the dusty sunlight" (*CS* 291). Perhaps O'Connor sees this image as presenting her readers with a newborn babe in the straw-filled manger ready after her trials to begin a new life in Christ. But the tension that develops between O'Connor's intended message and its overt form clashes here. By keeping her characters largely unspecified, and by focusing on ambiguous or neutral pronoun references or indefinite noun referents such as "the girl," O'Connor disengages herself from her characters, who are theologically important only as instruments through which God works. This stylistic technique seems to defeat her intense personal desire to deliver an audience antagonistic to a loving, caring, Catholic God into the religious society she feels they have rejected. Despite her detailed glosses, her language guides her readers away from her theological designs. The reader might rightly ask where is the linguistic message reinforcing the Christian directive "do unto others" or love of thy sister/brother, or that even the least of us is loved by God.

For over three chapters in *The Violent Bear It Away*, O'Connor refers to young Francis Marion Tarwater, when she names him, as Tarwater, and once she has him think of himself as F. M. Tarwater. It comes as some surprise, then, when Rayber, in chapter 4, addresses him as "Frankie." To this, Tarwater answers, "'And my name ain't Frankie. I go by Tarwater.'" (*Collected* 397). But Rayber is not concerned with Tarwater's objections. He continues to ignore Tarwater's wishes and from then on calls him "Frank." And even long after this incident, when he signs in at the Cherokee Lodge for their fishing trip, Rayber signs the check-in card with the names: "'George F. Rayber, Frank and Bishop Rayber'" (*Collected* 425). At this point, Tarwater becomes incensed and scratches out the name Rayber has given him replacing it with his full name, "Francis Marion Tarwater." Rayber, however, remains undaunted, and by the end of chapter 8, is still calling Tarwater "Frank." O'Connor seems to be insisting here that the being who sees his identity as Tarwater has little control over his own identification. Both she, as author, and Rayber, as her creation, effectively remove Tarwater's singularity and thwart his will by refusing to accept him as he requests to be accepted.

In "Everything That Rises Must Converge," Julian's mother, the focal point of the story, joins the long succession of O'Connor characters who have had their personal identities expunged. In *Invisible Parade: The Fiction of Flannery O'Connor*, Miles Orvell refers to Julian's mother as "Mrs. Chestny."[5] However, no such name is ever bestowed upon her in the story. O'Connor only refers to her as "Julian's mother," "his mother," or by pronominal references. Orvell has obviously reached conclusions about this character's identity from the following passages in this story:

> "Your great-grandfather was a former governor of this state," she said. "Your grandfather was a prosperous landowner. Your grandmother was a Godhigh."
>
> "I remember going to Grandpa's when I was a little girl. . . . Actually the place belonged to the Godhighs but your grandfather Chestny paid the mortgage and saved it for them. They were in reduced circumstances," she said, "but reduced or not, they never forgot who they were."
>
> All of her life had been a struggle to act like a Chestny without the Chestny goods, and to give him everything she thought a Chestny ought to have . . . (*CS* 407; 408; 411)

Julian's mother is reliving her childhood in these passages when the surname "Chestny" appears. Yet O'Connor's deliberate linguistic ambiguity about Julian's mother's ancestry effectively blurs Julian's mother's lineage. Whether "Chestny" could be Julian's mother's maiden name one can only speculate as "your grandfather Chestny" could refer to either Julian's mother's maternal or paternal relative. Orvell's title of "Mrs." would indicate that "Chestny" was Julian's mother's married name. Although "your grandfather Chestny" could conceivably have been Julian's father's father, we would then have to presume that this paternal grandfather was a beneficent man concerned enough about the finances of the family his son would eventually marry into that he would

---

[5]Miles Orvell, *Invisible Parade: The Fiction of Flannery O'Connor* (Philadelphia: Temple University Press, 1972) 4.

generously offer to pay their mortgage. This seems an imaginative stretch. O'Connor's references in these passages seem to be about Julian's mother's reminiscences about her own family's past wealth and her lack of it in her married life. If she had struggled "to act like a Chestny without the Chestny goods" does this not indicate that she had once been a Chestny but through marriage this status and its rewards had been lost? She had struggled to give Julian "everything she thought a Chestny ought to have" which implies that he is not a "Chestny." These facts, though ambiguous, corroborate the reality that Julian's mother cannot be "Mrs." Chestny as Orvell contends. She remains individually indistinct and personally invisible.

In truth, in this story, only three characters have names of their own: Julian; Caroline, his mother's childhood nurse who never appears in the story and is only mentioned in passing a few times; and Carver, the young black child who is most often referred to as "the little boy." The other characters are given no definite distinguishing personal names that would designate them as definite, separate, singular individuals. They are only: "the woman with the protruding teeth," "the woman with the canvas sandals," "the Negro," "a large gaily dressed, sullen-looking colored woman" who is also called "the woman," or "the Negress," or "the huge woman." While it is true that in the context of this story the characters on the bus would in all probability remain unknown to Julian and his mother, Julian's mother, around whom the plot pivots, is surely deserving of her own uniqueness, her own name. But she lives and dies nameless.

O'Connor also leaves nameless the two principal protagonists in "A Good Man Is Hard to Find." The grandmother of the story remains throughout, "the grandmother," or "the old lady." She is never addressed by any of the characters in the story by her given name and is only called "Mamma" once by Bailey, her son, at the moment he goes to his death. And "The Misfit" is always referred to as "The Misfit"; he even introduces himself as such. Curiously, O'Connor always capitalizes the article when she refers to him. It is true that use of the definite article "signals a *particular* person or thing that has been singled out from others."[6] Yet what O'Connor has singled out is an unnamed, disturbingly depraved pathological murderer who is called by *what* he is, not by *who* he is. This use of the definite article indicates that The Misfit, indeed, has a definite

[6]Marcella Frank, *Modern English: A Practical Reference Guide* (Englewood Cliffs, NJ: Prentice-Hall, Inc., 1972) 125.

identity, but one that the reader is obliged to associate with his crimes. He has no Christian name; it is his depravity that becomes specifically "incarnate" in O'Connor's world.

Yet O'Connor seemed surprised that in "A Good Man Is Hard to Find," in the minds of some of her audience at least, she appeared to be creating a world without God. She admonished her readers that they "should be on the lookout for such things as the action of grace in the Grandmother's soul, and not for the dead bodies" (*MM* 113). But can O'Connor's audience ignore the mass murders of an entire family, one of which is a sleeping baby? In a lecture she gave about this story, O'Connor detailed her views of the role she gave the two main characters. She considered The Misfit a "prophet gone wrong" who, because of the grandmother's actions, would turn into "the prophet he was meant to become" (*MM* 110; 113). And she expressed her dismay that she could be misread stating: "there are perhaps other ways than my own in which this story could be read, but none other by which it could have been written" (*MM* 109). Perhaps this statement too needed defending, for O'Connor's language with its persistence on camouflaging devices that conceal personal identities seems to insist on reading into her stories "the wrong horror."

Even when O'Connor does name a character, she employs several methods as cloaking devices to prevent the name from signaling any intimate personal attachment to a character. She distances readers from her characters by referring to them by last names or names that sound like last names: Sheppard, Johnson, Norton (in "The Lame Shall Enter First"); and Tanner and Coleman (in "Judgement Day"). In this last story Tanner's first name is reported two different ways: "T. C. Tanner" and later "W. T. Tanner" (*CS* 531; 542). Sally Fitzgerald explains this away as one of "a list of typographical errors corrected" in her notes at the back of *Collected Works*, and she makes the change to "T. C." in the reprinting of "Judgement Day" (*Collected* 1263). But to label this problem with character identification as a typographical error seems to gloss over the fact that throughout O'Connor's fiction, names are only important as they emblematically or allegorically impact the plotline. There is, of course, no way to determine absolutely the origin of the change in initials. However, mistakenly striking the keys "W" and "T" instead of the keys "T" and "C" on a typewriter during the creation of the story would be difficult to accomplish accidently for any typist. It would also seem farfetched to assume that at the typesetting stage this particular transposition could have taken place. The fact that O'Connor may not have noticed this mistake during the various stages of revisions, however, may be entirely possible as she was revising this story during her last illness in 1964 and may have been distracted from her usual conscientiousness. But the end result of this printing "error" seems compatible with O'Connor's naming techniques throughout her writing career. Names for purposes other than as instructional devices through which her message would be reinforced always held little import for O'Connor, a fact which probably contributed to her failure to notice that she had Tanner sign his notes with these two very different sets of initials.

O'Connor seemed most comfortable using names allegorically or emblematically to emphasize an aspect of a character's frailty seen essential to her message. For example Mrs. Hopewell of "Good Country People" always hopes for the best. Sheppard of "The Lame Shall Enter First" thinks of himself as the savior of Rufus Johnson and, therefore, must have had a connection in O'Connor's mind with the "Shepherd-Savior" Christ. And Hazel Motes in *Wise Blood*, most often referred to as Haze, is allegorically twice blessed, his last name indicating a speck of dust or ash in the eye, and his first name indicating the haze through which he sees reality until he completes the allegory by self-blinding.

Many other naming examples indicate O'Connor's desire to minimize the individualities of her characters. In "The Life You Save May Be Your Own" O'Connor uses names to demean personalities: Lucynell Crater's surname signifies her lack of intellectual capabilities, and Mr. Tom T. Shiftlet's surname symbolizes his lack of character. Type names for O'Connor can also indicate the opposite of their customary meaning: Joy in "Good Country People" has none, Mr. Paradise in "The River" does not believe in any, and Mr. Fortune of "A View of the Woods" loses his after he kills his granddaughter who had been his very life, his only fortune. By her avoidance of individual personalities and her creation of characters who only exhibit types, O'Connor textually obliterates the human beings she so carefully creates. For O'Connor, the message intentionally overshadows the messenger. Impersonality in her treatment of character types forces O'Connor's audience away from any concern for the fates of her characters and often reduces to a ridiculing humor the vagaries of their souls.

O'Connor's resistance toward breathing an individual soul into her fictional characters has often caused her readers and some of her critics to fail to perceive her message as Christian, let alone Catholic. O'Connor herself was aware that her style did not always achieve its intended mark. She wrote to "A" in 1955, of a criticism she had received:

> H. Motes was not human enough to sustain his [George Clay's] interest. . . . However, his interesting comment was that the best of my work sounded like the Old Testament would sound if it were being written today—in as much (partly) as the character's relation is directly with God rather than with other people. He points out, correctly, that it is hard to sustain the reader's interest in a character like that unless he is very human. I am trying to make this new novel more human, less farcial [sic]. A great strain for me. (*Collected* 963)

Unfortunately, O'Connor never seemed able to contend with this stylistic adversary. Her characters, despite her attention to descriptive detail, never draw out her compassion. They remain archetypes of those fallen from grace; O'Connor's language does not afford them considerations as individual souls tainted by original sin yet capable of redemption by a merciful God. O'Connor's linguistic sketches greatly undermine the Catholic doctrine she espouses by presenting a brutal, exacting deity demanding total submission, a departure from the New Testament God who is compassionately mindful of the weaknesses of his creatures. Although O'Connor's writing gets praise from Martha Stephens "for her cunning selection of detail and delicate sense for nuance in speech and manners, and for the wonderfully controlled momentum with which her stories move," her style remains problematically rigid and forced.[7] O'Connor's effectiveness as a writer does lie in her ability to create vivid, if mean-spirited, characterizations and in her immense storytelling competence, but the theological intentions that her characters must address if O'Connor's message is to be read as Catholic are deeply buried beneath an annihilating language that hides from the reader any overt Catholic relevance.

An analysis of O'Connor's grammatical constructions demonstrates how redemptively paralyzing her language is. Zelda Boyd, in her work "The Grammar of Representation in Psychoanalysis and Literature," considers that "grammatical forms can have meaning and that the use of a particular form is to some degree a discretionary choice about how this

---

[7]Martha Stephens, *The Question of Flannery O'Connor* (Baton Rouge: Louisiana State University, 1973) 11.

event is to be represented and where the speaker is to be placed in relation to it."[8] She agrees with Freud's assertions in his essay, "A Child Is Being Beaten" that the use of the "generic" subject and the passive construction permits a distancing of both the subject as well as the agent of the action.[9] Boyd continues her observations by stating that:

> English offers many ways of avoiding agency besides the passive construction. . . . Consider . . . "the impulse seized me," which reverses the conceptual agent through metaphor, or consider sentences like "the twig snapped," "the water boiled," which are neither passives nor conventional actor/action sentences but happenings, i.e., events represented without reference to an agent or cause . . .[10]

With these examples Boyd explains that a writer is able to produce an agentless condition by means other than the obvious use of the passive voice, a stylistic arrangement often used by O'Connor.

In her fiction, O'Connor frequently chooses adjectives that have passive intent. These adjectives are constructed from the past participle or "-en" form of the verb and are referred to as "passive participial adjective[s]" by Cluett.[11] In the story "Greenleaf" O'Connor describes the bull as "silvered in the moonlight" with "his head raised" (*CS* 311). The use of "silvered" indicates passivity on the part of the agent, literally, the moon, and the adjective "raised" implies that the subject "head" was acted upon rather than being the initiator of the action. Here, O'Connor, by positioning the bull as receiver of the action, sets up a rhetorical condition making the bull a passive instrument selected by God—hence "silvered" and "raised." The bull becomes one of O'Connor's many controlled beings denied any freedom of choice, any free will. Instead he has his deific role imposed upon him by O'Connor's language.

Later in the same paragraph, O'Connor writes that "Clouds crossing the moon blackened him." While the sentence structure is overtly active voice, O'Connor suggests a passive intent since the bull, the "him" of the sentence, is the receiver of the action initiated by the clouds. Continuing

---

[8]Zelda Boyd, "The Grammar of Representation in Psychoanalysis and Literature," in *The Psychoanalytic Study of Literature*, ed. Reppen and Charney, 114.

[9]Ibid., 113.

[10]Ibid., 116.

[11]Robert Cluett, *Prose Style and Critical Reading* (New York: Teachers College Press, 1976) 87.

to describe the bull, O'Connor writes that "Bars of light slid across him as the venetian blind was slit" (*CS* 311). Both of these examples fall into the category of Boyd's "happenings," where the bull, a Christ-figure in this O'Connor story, is acted upon by celestial elements (the moon, the clouds, the light). Because of the passive intent of this sentence structure, the bull is implicitly designated as anointed by God on high for his future role in Mrs. May's redemption. Active participation in these events and decisions remains out of the bull's control because of O'Connor's linguistic choices. Additionally, the use of "was slit" in the sentence quoted above is a true passive with the agent remaining unexpressed, a grammatical construction used when the "doer of an action is unimportant or is not known."[12] This language syntactically removes the action from Mrs. May's direct control. Mrs. May is the obvious operator of the venetian blind since it is in her bedroom window where it hangs, so it is logical to consider O'Connor's passive construction an indication of personal unimportance.

O'Connor's use of passive voice, passive participial adjectives, and her proclivity for rendering subjects invisible draws her focus away from the agency of her characters and places the action in control of an unnamed Other, which we can only assume is God. The stylistic implications of these writing techniques point toward an interpretation of free will that seems Calvinist in doctrine and that causes a variety of differing interpretations of O'Connor's works. *The Catholic Encyclopedia* summarizes the free will philosophy of Calvinism as perceived by Catholics:

> Man can perform no sort of good act unless necessitated to it by God's grace, which it [sic] is impossible for him to resist. It is absurd to speak of the human will "co-operating" with God's grace, for this would imply that man could resist the grace of God.[13]

The Catholic viewpoint, in variance with Calvinism, gave formal response to this doctrine through the Council of Trent:

---

[12]Frank, *Modern English*, 56.

[13]Michael Maher, "Free Will," in *The Catholic Encyclopedia,* 15 vols., ed. Herberhann, et al., 6: 261.

> The will can resist grace if it chooses. It is not like a lifeless thing, which remains purely passive. Weakened and diminished by Adam's fall, free will is not yet destroyed in the race.[14]

O'Connor addresses her ideas of free will in *Mystery and Manners.*

> My view of free will follows the traditional Catholic teaching. I don't think any genuine novelist is interested in writing about a world of people who are strictly determined. Even if he writes about characters who are mostly unfree, it is the sudden free action, the open possibility, which he knows is the only thing capable of illuminating the picture and giving it life. So that while predictable, predetermined actions have a comic interest for me, it is the free act, the acceptance of grace particularly, that I always have my eye on as the thing which will make the story work. (*MM* 115)

O'Connor's language choices seem, however unconsciously, to contradict her statement and keep her stories from working in the way she intended. The people in her world are, in actuality, predetermined by her linguistic choices. O'Connor's passive language and lack of agency leave her characters unable to act on their own accord. How can her characters exhibit the free will to choose or reject what God offers them if they are rendered impotent at the literal level by O'Connor's language choices? And even if O'Connor's language would allow her characters to act, most readers, expecting to find Catholicism in the free acceptance of grace, would have difficulty believing that the grandmother in "A Good Man Is Hard to Find" would choose her grace in her own murder and the murder of her family. O'Connor may have intended freedom of choice for her characters, but the grammatical forms she chooses imply otherwise.

Additionally, an investigation of O'Connor's verb selections serves to corroborate a fictional atmosphere lacking in freedom of choice. O'Connor's verbs express lethargy and inaction on the part of her fictional characters. In story after story, her characters, unable to find their purpose in life, sit or stand, stare or gaze, and wait for something or someone to act upon them. Mr. Head in "The Artificial Nigger" "sat up and stared at the floor boards." (*CS* 249). Mrs. Freeman in "Good Country People" "would stand there and if she could be brought to say anything, it was

---

[14]Ibid.

something like, 'Well, I wouldn't of said it was and I wouldn't of said it wasn't'" (*CS* 271). And Mrs. May in "Greenleaf," immersed in the ultimate apathy,

> remained perfectly still, not in fright, but in a freezing unbelief. She stared at the violent black streak bounding toward her as if she had no sense of distance, as if she could not decide at once what his intention was, and the bull had buried his head in her lap, like a wild tormented lover, before her expression changed. (CS 333)

O'Connor is continually emphasizing her characters' incapacity for action on their own accord. Yet in Catholic theology, "man really co-operates in his personal salvation from sin."[15] Most of O'Connor's characters, however, like Mrs. May, passively wait to be acted upon by a vengeful god-figure before their expressions are allowed to change, and they are given their moments of grace. O'Connor's verb choices once again imply a world at variance with her expressed views on free will and the free acceptance of grace, and with the Catholic concept of salvation. And Catholic doctrine notwithstanding, it becomes problematical to reconcile O'Connor's message with her theology when the action of grace that is allowed Mrs. May is a brutal goring by a bull, hardly the method any sane and rational being would voluntarily choose or the Lamb of God of the New Testament would gently sanction.

O'Connor also employs a multitude of linguistic modal auxiliaries such as "might," "would," "could," and "should," which Boyd indicates "are marked as a class for uncertainty."[16] In "The Lame Shall Enter First" when Sheppard finally realizes that he had ignored the well-being of his own child, O'Connor from this point onward refers to Sheppard pronominally and reports his thoughts about his child with conditional statements:

> He would make everything up to him. He would never let him suffer again. He would be mother and father. He jumped up and ran to his room, to kiss him, to tell him that he loved him, that he would never fail him again. (*CS* 482)

---

[15]A. J. Maas, "Salvation," in *The Catholic Encyclopedia*, 15 vols., ed. Herberhann, et al., 13: 408.

[16]Boyd, "The Grammar of Representation," 119.

While the conditional modal "would" suggests possibility, it also permits the possibility of negation. In fact, Sheppard will never be able to carry out his desires for by the time he reaches the attic, Norton has hanged himself. Sheppard will never be able to make up for his past sins. O'Connor does not allow him a Catholic absolution for past wrongs. Sheppard may repent of his wicked ways, but O'Connor's God does not hear confessions. Where is Sheppard's "sudden free action," his "open possibility" that O'Connor wrote about in *Mystery and Manners* (115)? Instead, Sheppard is thoroughly controlled through the use of pronouns and use of the conditional past tense and effectively exterminated as a spiritual being able to participate in the choosing of grace. His world of "would be's" mandates his imposed impotency, while the impact of his revelation leaves him alone and hurting with only an awakened sense of spiritual uncertainties and impossibilities. O'Connor continually forces this same message in her thematic considerations and reinforces it through her premeditated stylistic techniques.

That O'Connor's stories follow a linguistic formula seems evident in many instances throughout her fiction. In "The Lame Shall Enter First," *The Violent Bear It Away*, *Wise Blood*, "Revelation," and "Good Country People," O'Connor amazingly has almost the same number of verbs on the first page of each work (for uniformity the first 319 words of each were analyzed). Use of the copula, which is the "verb *to be* when functioning as the main verb," emphasizes a state of being rather than action and shifts focus back to the subject by functioning as a link between subject and complement, and "be" is heavily represented in O'Connor's stories.[17] Linking verbs (in which category "be" is included) are also very much in evidence in these stories. As Marcella Frank states, "A linking verb is a verb of incomplete predication; it merely announces that the real predicate follows."[18] Frank lists the most common linking verbs as: "**appear, be, become, get** (in the sense of **become**), **look, remain, seem** . . . [and] the verbs of perception—**feel, taste, smell, sound**" as well as "**behold, . . . hear, listen to, notice, observe, perceive, see, watch, witness**."[19] When all linking verbs are counted in the O'Connor stories men-

[17]Elizabeth Closs Traugott and Mary Louise Pratt, *Linguistics for Students of Literature* (New York: Harcourt Brace Jovanovich, 1980) 402.

[18]Frank, *Modern English*, 309.

[19]Ibid., 48, 309.

tioned above their percentages in each work (except for *The Violent Bear It Away*) are astonishingly similar.

WORK:	# OF VERBS	% OF "BE"	% LINKING VERBS
"The Lame Shall Enter First"	42	19%	33%
The Violent Bear It Away	44	20%	23%
Wise Blood	45	16%	31%
"Revelation"	48	23%	31%
"Good Country People"	50	24%	30%

There seems a consistency in O'Connor's verb patterning here and throughout her fiction. She uses the copula and other linking verbs, a choice that forces stagnation upon her characters. Her verb choices work in conjunction with her use of passive voice to remove the action from the subject's direct control.[20]

Furthermore, O'Connor's verb tenses appear to reinforce the same message of inertia she has subtly conveyed through the use of the copula and other linking verbs. She chooses mostly past, past progressive, past perfect, and conditional past tense verb constructions for her fiction. The progressive tense is most pertinent to maintaining stagnation as its use contributes greatly to O'Connor's character restrictions. In her discussion of tense and aspect that "the English verb most readily expresses through the progressive forms of the tenses,"[21] Boyd writes:

> Aspect involves not only inclusion and exclusion, presence and absence; it also segments events in relation to the beginning, the duration, or the conclusion. . . . Certain of our verb forms, like the progressive—"I am reading," "I was running"—preserve the durative sense . . .[22]

As Boyd views it, the use of the progressive tense allows an author "to avoid completed acts."[23] O'Connor's verbal usage routinely relies on the past progressive tense, symbolically placing her characters in a limbo-like setting. In "A Good Man Is Hard to Find" the grandmother "was seizing at every chance to change Bailey's mind." Bailey (who, unlike the

[20]See pages 23-24 for discussion of passive voice.

[21]Frank, *Modern English*, 47.

[22]Boyd, "The Grammar of Representation," 118.

[23]Ibid.

grandmother, does merit a name in this story) "was sitting on the edge of his chair" while his wife (called "the children's mother") "was sitting on the sofa," and the children, John Wesley and June Star, "were reading the funny papers" (*CS* 117). This tense choice parallels the worldly existences of these characters with their spiritual existences. The past progressive tense sustains their status as spiritual nonentities searching for but never reaching their goals.

O'Connor's lexical choices of verbs are as limiting as her tense choices. The following list from the first paragraph of "Good Country People" illustrates O'Connor's simple yet deadening verb style:

> wore, was, had, used, was, swerved, turned, turned, followed, used, was not, to retract, did, came, was, seemed, would see, stand, was, was, had given up, might talk, could never be brought to admit, would stand, could be brought to say, was, wouldn't of said it was, wouldn't of said it wasn't, range, was, might remark, see, ain't ate, put up. (*CS* 271)

These familiar and even colloquial verb forms prepare the reader for recognizable realities of a culture presumably shared. Yet the readers are jolted into a macabre view of reality in total opposition to the world O'Connor's verbal choices guided them to see. O'Connor's comments about the vision of a fictional writer is pertinent to how her readers respond to her stylistic choices:

> The kind of vision the fiction writer needs to have, or to develop, in order to increase the meaning of his story is called anagogical vision, and that is the kind of vision that is able to see different levels of reality in one image or one situation. (*MM* 72)

One of the different levels produced by O'Connor's conventional verb choices and verb forms invites her readers to envision a world with which they are acquainted. Yet the action that occurs in most O'Connor stories emanates from a freakish world in which unfamiliar religious meanings are hidden from sight through conventional language usages.

O'Connor's stylistic choices constantly hinder her efforts to disseminate her Catholic message to her reading public. She continually utilizes writing techniques that so successfully veil any visage of Catholic doctrine that her readers, confused about the fate of her characters' souls and impeded in their attempts to perceive her stated Catholic intent, often fail to perceive O'Connor's anagogical vision as containing an embracement of her religion. Stylistically through sentence structure, parts of speech, naming techniques, and verb usage, O'Connor disallows intimacy with her fictional creations and removes from them the ability to act on their own accord. Grace for O'Connor is not offered; it is decreed. O'Connor's linguistic extermination and determinism place her fictional environment into the very same world in which Boyd places Nick in Hemingway's "The Killers":

> It is a world of happenings set in motion by some unnamed and perhaps unknowable power and events follow in mindless succession with a terrible depersonalized inevitability.[24]

O'Connor's linguistic choices infuse and even overtake her message creating a narrative detachment from her characters so thoroughly pervasive that the resulting fictional product works against any convictions she may have that souls are worth saving, that God's creatures may freely choose or reject his grace, or that her God is one of love or compassion.

---

[24]Ibid., 122.

2.
Symbolic Barriers to Salvation

On 28 October 1960, at a Wesleyan College symposium in Macon, Georgia, O'Connor stated the following:

> I really didn't know what a symbol was until I started reading about them. It seemed I was going to have to know about them if I was going to be a respectable literary person. Now I have the notion that a symbol is sort of like the engine in a story and I usually discover as I write something in the story that is taking on more and more meaning so that as I go along, before long, that something is turning or working the story.[1]

While some of Flannery O'Connor's symbols can be easily translated from thing to concept, many spring peculiarly from O'Connor's eccentric imagination. The bizarre and often forced meanings she perceived as capturing her Christian message create a variety of interpretations and are often misunderstood by her audience which has not been adequately prepared by the prose or has been misguided by internal textual inconsistencies.

Eugene Nida states that "a symbol is an instrument by which we label and manipulate our conceptions. In other words, it is the conceptions, not the things, that symbols directly 'mean.'"[2] However, Nida also states that "problems of communication arise largely because essentially the same symbols may have radically different meanings."[3] While Nida intended the confusion of radically different symbolic meanings to indicate a variance of meanings from author to author, O'Connor's symbols vary from story to story, a condition that places an added burden upon the reader to decipher her actual intent.

Undoubtedly O'Connor used symbolism as the core around which she structured her work. She would, however, disavow the symbolic meaning on occasion as this recollection in her letter to Charlotte Gafford suggests:

---

[1]Melvin J. Friedman and Lewis A. Lawson, *The Added Dimension: The Art and Mind of Flannery O'Connor* (New York: Fordham University Press, 1966) 8.

[2]Eugene A. Nida, *Message and Mission: The Communication of the Christian Faith* (New York: Harper & Brothers Publishers, 1960) 66.

[3]Ibid., 1.

> They try to make everything a symbol. It kills me. At one place where I talked, one of them said, "Miss O'Connor, why was the Misfit's hat **black**?" "Well," I said, "he stold [sic] it from a countryman and in Georgia they usually wear black hats." This sounded like a pretty stupid answer to him, but he wasn't through with it. In a few minutes he says, "Miss O'Connor, what is the significance of the Misfit's hat?" "To cover his head," I say. (*HB* 465)

Yet, O'Connor is insistent on the control an author must have and states this unequivocally when she writes in "The Nature and Aim of Fiction" that

> The novelist makes his statements by selection, and if he is any good, he selects every word for a reason, every detail for a reason, every incident for a reason, and arranges them in a certain time-sequence for a reason. (*MM* 75)

Considering this last statement, then, as her sense of a writer's obligation, we can assume that O'Connor's use of two familiar symbols, the sun and hats (especially black hats) do have an intended meaning.

Mary Parr, in a book review of J. Mitchell Morse discussing the question of James Joyce's Catholicism, makes a statement that bears directly on Flannery O'Connor's use of symbolism. She writes:

> St. Thomas is saying the active intellect in man according to Aristotle is like the light received into the air, or, as in Plato, like the sun which furnishes the light. In St. Thomas we go beyond comparison into causality: the active intellect in man is not only like that light and that sun but this intellect in man is caused by God as are the light and the sun. It is not "God Himself"; it is something in man; it is the power of understanding; it is man's divinity. Joyce knew this. His art is an attempt to lift the shadow that man has cast about his own active intellect.[4]

O'Connor's art, however, makes little attempt to lift that shadow. In fact, her symbolic treatment seems a strategy intent on subterfuge.

---

[4]Mary Parr, "James Joyce and Catholicism," in *Renascence: A Critical Journal of Letters* 13/2 (Winter 1961): 106.

Repeatedly in O'Connor's fiction the light and sun appear as symbols for God, but if in her stories her characters partake of "the power of understanding" and "man's divinity," she blurs this through an unorthodox symbolic system. Her symbols, like her grammatical choices, generate a bewildering religious paradox and undergo constant fluctuations. Her characters, caught in this symbolic upheaval, often become spiritually paralyzed able only to see but not to act. They are rendered unable or unwilling to participate actively in a quest toward divinity. In fact, O'Connor feels that "Human nature is so faulty that it can resist any amount of grace and most of the time it does" (*Collected* 1084). The operative word is "can" here, but O'Connor's characters "cannot." O'Connor removes from them the opportunity to resist grace (an option absolutely open to Catholics) by creating characters who are symbolically unable to select from the choices the Christian faith affords them. Her characters remain mired, instead, in the sins of their forbearers powerless by her symbols to make a decision between salvation and damnation. O'Connor's symbolic choices extend the inactivity already imposed on them by her grammatical constructions. This enforced symbolic and linguistic impotency visited on the spirituality of her characters establishes little overt Catholicism in the textuality of her stories leaving the reader puzzling over whether her characters can or do achieve salvation.

O'Connor's usage of the sun as symbol in her stories would seem familiar to readers as the sun is universally regarded as representing creative power. O'Connor, however, links this commonly understood symbol with uncharacteristic couplings. In the following description from her story "A Temple of the Holy Ghost," she makes the explicit symbolic connection of sun as God when she writes:

> The sun was a huge red ball like an elevated Host drenched in blood and when it sank out of sight, it left a line in the sky like a red clay road hanging over the trees. (*CS* 248)

But perhaps because of her theological conviction that "All human nature vigorously resists grace," O'Connor seldom allows the sun to shine directly on her characters (*Collected* 1084). In her stories she equips her fictional personalities with interminable protection by shielding them from God's light by some physical object or impediment. In general, O'Connor uses hats as physical barriers prohibiting the sun, or God, from touching those who remain unsaved, while their hatless counterparts are allowed to become part of the chosen few. Her characters very often wear hats, many times black hats, and these frequently support wide brims which shade the eyes of her protagonists, symbolically preventing them from receiving grace.

Hats as symbolic obstacles are ubiquitous in O'Connor's fiction. The Bible salesman in "Good Country People," when he first visits the Hopewell family as the innocent Manley Pointer, is described as a "tall gaunt hatless youth" (*CS* 277). When the Bible salesman meets Joy-Hulga with the intent to violate her, O'Connor has him outfitted with a "hat which was new and wide-brimmed" (*CS* 285). She reinforces the importance of the Bible salesman's hat by indicating that "He had not worn it yesterday and she [Hulga] wondered if he had bought it for the occasion" (*CS* 285). Indeed, he has brought it for the occasion, for it will provide him, as one of O'Connor's unsaved characters, with a barrier to the all-present sunshine available to the potentially saveable Hulga who has "A wide sheath of sunlight, filled with dust particles, slanted over her"; he will be allowed to sin in the shadows (*CS* 287). As the two begin their attempts at mutually seducing each other, "The sky was cloudless and cold blue" and able to permit a glance toward the Almighty for both characters (*CS* 287). Yet O'Connor makes sure the Bible salesman "did not remove his hat." Instead, "it was pushed far enough back not to interfere" (*CS* 287). He could push it back so that it would not interfere with his attempts to seduce Hulga, but he would not remove it so that it would interfere with any attempts from God to overtake his soul.

The acknowledged heroine in "Good Country People," Hulga, wears no hat, and she should not if we can trust O'Connor's hat symbols, for she is capable of salvation. But the Bible salesman, whose purpose is to be the foil off which Hulga plays, does wear a hat, and so he should since he assumes the role of devil in this scenario. Hats are so vital to O'Connor's message that she leaves the Bible salesman with one last reference to her all powerful symbol: "and then the toast-colored hat disappeared down the hole and the girl was left, sitting on the straw in the dusty sunlight" (*CS* 291). Hulga, the redeemed, remains hatless so that potentially she may stake a claim on O'Connor's promise of sunlight. The hatted Bible salesman, as one of O'Connor's damned, retains his hat—actively refusing access to the light and sun believed by St. Thomas to infuse man with divinity.

In "A Good Man Is Hard to Find" several characters wear hats or head coverings. The grandmother wears a "navy blue straw sailor hat with a bunch of white violets on the brim" (*CS* 118). The children's mother has "her head tied around in a green head-kerchief that had two points on the top like a rabbit's ears" (*CS* 117). The Misfit wears a black hat, and Hiram, one of the killers, wears a gray hat. O'Connor makes enough references to these head coverings for the reader to be fully conscious of their importance as symbol. While a jaunty sailor hat with artificial flowers adorning it or an absurd looking rabbit-eared kerchief make her characters appear ridiculous, O'Connor never trivializes the black or gray hats mentioned without further comment in connection with two of the characters, The Misfit and Hiram, who will later commit murder. The type of hat O'Connor gives a character takes on symbolic meaning.

When the grandmother's unfortunate family first encounters the three criminals, The Misfit is *holding* his hat, yet by the time he kills the grandmother he had "put on his black hat" (*CS* 129). If O'Connor writes "every word for a reason," then we as readers can safely assume that *holding* the hat must have had significance in her mind, as does the fact that The Misfit put the hat on again after committing murder. O'Connor seems to be indicating that The Misfit, *sans* hat, as one of God's own, is exposed to grace, but once he actively places the hat properly on his head, he can rightfully and vigorously reject grace. This black hat-armor seems able to provide him the appropriate shield to withstand that fierce O'Connor sun-God who frequently thrusts salvation upon his creatures, willing or not.

O'Connor furnishes additional reinforcement of hats as shields from God's light and saving grace by having Hiram, the killer-companion, pull Bailey up to take him to the woods for slaughter, while his partner Bobby Lee (who is never described as wearing a hat) only follows. It is also Hiram whom The Misfit instructs to take the children's mother into the woods, and while Bobby Lee does pull June Star along with him, O'Connor makes it clear that these two went "into the woods after Hiram and her mother," putting Hiram, the hatted criminal in the role of primary killer and hat-shielded sinner (*CS* 131). O'Connor's symbols, thus far, seem consistent in this story and in "Good Country People."

The sun and hats consistently appear together as combined symbols in O'Connor's work. Further examination of "A Good Man Is Hard to Find" discloses that when The Misfit is without his hat, he seems searching in the cloudless sky for the sun or God and says, "Don't see no sun but don't see no cloud neither" (*CS* 127). When the grandmother says to him "I just know you're a good man," however, The Misfit responds "Nome, I ain't a good man," and before that paragraph is over O'Connor writes that "He put on his black hat" (*CS* 128; 129). We can only assume the black hat remains on his head during the grandmother's murder as no mention is made of it again. The relevance of hats as baffles interfering with the redeeming grace-rays emanating through the sun of God is strengthened when the reader notices that The Misfit, after putting on his hat, never again makes a direct reference to the sun. Instead, O'Connor only writes that he "looked up suddenly," and after he expounds on his frustrated life she once more has him "looking up again at the cloudless sky" (*CS* 129; 130). The Misfit, her "prophet gone wrong," when equipped with his hat, no longer verbalizes about the existence of the sun, O'Connor's symbolic substitute for God. The reader, extrapolating information gleaned from previously read stories such as "Good Country People" might easily conclude that wearing a hat surely relegates one to the ranks of those unsaved sinners who would not be seeking the grace of God. However, the hat symbol, which seems to suggest damnation for the Bible salesman and for Hiram, one of the killers in "A Good Man" apparently does not effect the same meaning for The Misfit. For despite The Misfit's connections with hats and his disassociation with the sun, O'Connor has often stated that he is potentially capable of attaining salvation. In truth, in her estimation, The Misfit possesses more capacity for grace than the grandmother (*MM* 111).

Given O'Connor's comments about the redemptive potential of the two main characters from "A Good Man Is Hard to Find," the reader comparing the grandmother's symbolic treatment and The Misfit's discovers interesting discrepancies. O'Connor frequently indicates the prominence of the sky and the sun in the world of both of these characters. She states again after the grandmother is left alone with her killer that "There was not a cloud in the sky nor any sun. There was nothing around her but woods" (*CS* 131). At this point in the story, none of O'Connor's characters has received the saving grace of God, and the sun is absent from their world. However, the grandmother, after she realizes the terrible predicament her family is in, is symbolically able to search for God by becoming virtually hatless because O'Connor pointedly indicates that after the car accident her hat brim "came off in her hand" (*CS* 128). The grandmother, then, while she does still wear her hat, has no protrusion to hinder her vision. Does this mean she accepts her moment of grace since the sun can now shine into her soul?

Kathleen Feeley writes that for Flannery O'Connor "recognition is the first step toward truth, which is, in turn, the necessary condition of Redemption."[5] The grandmother does voluntarily reach out to The Misfit in recognition, but through this action O'Connor only allows her to become aware of salvation. She has precious little time to make a rational, conscious decision for the moment she touches The Misfit O'Connor writes that he "sprang back as if a snake had bitten him and shot her three times through the chest" (*CS* 132). O'Connor leaves the grandmother at the instant of her death gazing toward the sun with "her face smiling up at the cloudless sky" (*CS* 132). No mention is made of the sun, but all obstacles to receiving God's grace have been removed. Her recognition of herself and her own sins in the crazed criminal who kills her does not presuppose that the grandmother has accepted the violent term of the grace forced upon her. Readers attempting to rely on O'Connor's symbols for a determination of her salvation can only be uncertain as to O'Connor's symbolic meaning. The hat symbol should indicate the grandmother's ability to become saved, but why is there no mention of the sun in her dying world? She seems only able to share the same cloudless world of The Misfit which he possesses when he commits the mortal sin against God's Commandment, "Thou shalt not kill." It would appear that the unreliability of O'Connor's symbols explains, at least in part, the plethora of conflicting critical interpretations of O'Connor's actual fictional intent.

In her two novels, O'Connor also employs hat symbolism which presumably follows the overt pattern of her short stories: characters seem to wear hats while unsaved but become hatless when saved. Throughout *The Violent Bear It Away* Young Tarwater clings to his hat. O'Connor writes: "He followed his uncle's custom of never taking off his hat except in bed" (*Collected* 337). Tarwater, her reluctant prophet, must find a substitute head covering when his hat falls as he looks out the lawyer's window. Symbolically, his head must be covered before he can venture out of the lawyer's office into the sunlight; he has still not accepted his destiny and, therefore, must cover his head to keep from being accessible to God's grace. So, when he leaves the office O'Connor reports that, "He

[5]Kathleen Feeley, *Flannery O'Connor: Voice of the Peacock* (New Brunswick: Rutgers University Press, 1972) 23.

had an old work kerchief tied around his head, knotted at the four corners" (*Collected* 348).

Tarwater's head remains covered throughout the novel until he meets his moment of truth when the villainous stranger (also wearing a hat) violates him. O'Connor symbolically reinforces the newly defenseless Tarwater's right to redemption by removing the hat-shield from him when the stranger sneaks away from his sadistic crime "carrying the boy's hat for a souvenir" (*Collected* 472). At this point in the story "When Tarwater woke up, the sun was directly overhead, very small and silver, sifting down light that seemed to spend itself before it reached him" (*Collected* 472). As Tarwater regains his senses "He perceived that his hat was gone" (*Collected* 472). Hatless, he should soon be ready to be infused with grace to make him the prophet his uncle groomed him to be.

O'Connor writes to John Hawkes on 26 December 1959: "It is the violation in the woods that brings home to Tarwater the real nature of his rejection. I couldn't have brought off the final vision without it" (*Collected* 1119). If O'Connor considers Young Tarwater a prophet (and from all indications in her letters he achieves that status), why does she describe the sun when it first has the opportunity to enter his soul as "small" with a "light that *seemed* to *spend* itself before it reached him" [my emphasis]? If one needs the sun to receive grace (the grandmother died looking for it; Hulga was bathed in it), and if one must be hatless to be available for grace, why would the sun's saving rays be all but exhausted before they can reach a young hatless Tarwater? What obviously should be O'Connor's signal to her readers that Tarwater's moment of grace is at hand and that finally he is able to receive it (for this is the symbolic pattern she elsewhere employs, and this seems her intent as evinced by her comments to Hawkes), instead becomes a confusion of language choices and symbolic inconsistencies.

Neither hat symbols nor the symbolic treatment of the sun in connection with Old Tarwater corresponds with symbolic patterns attached to other characters within the novel nor with previous patterns developed in other short stories. For Young Tarwater, the hat symbolism remains consistent with that used in "Good Country People." But this is not the case with Tarwater's great-uncle. Old Tarwater dies inside the house at the breakfast table with his hat on: "a putty-colored hat with the brim turned up" (*Collected* 335). If Young Tarwater needs to be hatless to experience grace, is Old Tarwater with his head covered, even in death, one of the damned? In an earlier letter to John Hawkes on 13 September

1959, however, O'Connor declares Old Tarwater a prophet (*Collected* 1107). Perhaps, then, having his hat brim turned up puts him in the same category as the grandmother in "A Good Man Is Hard to Find": hatted, but because the brim has been removed or diminished, able to receive the saving light of God. It becomes perplexing, nevertheless, that Tarwater, whom we can assume is saved based on O'Connor's comments, dies inside the house in a kitchen "large and dark" (*Collected* 335). The sun's light, which seemed so necessary for Hulga and the grandmother and which is at least mentioned in connection with Young Tarwater's moment of grace, is apparently not necessary at all for Old Tarwater's salvation. Also troubling in determining O'Connor's symbolic intent is that the symbolic action that precedes the removal of Young Tarwater's hat and opens him to the availability of grace, is a homosexual rape. Readers expecting to see grace realized in New Testament terms by a benevolent God are introduced, instead, to rapes and murders as the conduits connecting redemption to the redeemed.

O'Connor's conception of the state necessary for an individual soul to attain redemption also deviates from common Catholic/Christian beliefs. When Tarwater accepts a ride from the stranger who is the "actualization of Tarwater's friend and mentor, the Devil" (*Collected* 1119), he utters four significant statements:

> "I drowned a boy."
>
> "I baptized him."
>
> "It was an accident."
>
> "I only meant to drown him, . . ." (*Collected* 458)

The accident, in Tarwater's mind, was not the drowning; it was the baptism. In Catholic theology, even the sin of murder can be forgiven. The requirements are: disclosure of the sin either directly to God or to a priest in the confessional with the stipulation that absolution of the sin is contingent on the penitent's true sorrow for the offense against God; a sincere resolve to refrain from repeating the offense; and reparation through some form of penance. Tarwater meets none of these conditions. He "confesses" his sin to the devil, but the confession is nothing more than a retelling of an event; he never repents of his murder of Bishop, and he does no penance to atone for his sinful action. Yet, Tarwater remains blameless of sin in O'Connor's assessment:

> That murder is forgotten by God and of no interest to society, and I would proceed quickly to show what the children of God do to him. I am much more interested in the nobility of unnaturalness than in the nobility of naturalness. (*Collected* 1101)

To thrust grace forcefully upon hapless, helpless, creatures like Bishop, by drowning; and on sinful, fanatical, remorseless creatures like Tarwater, by a brutal rape is uncharacteristic of the God O'Connor's Catholic audience would worship. Because O'Connor's God is a wrathful, Old Testament Yahweh who victimizes the weak and considers "unnaturalness" noble, there is little wonder that readers often dispute the spiritual disposition of the souls of her characters, a disputation made even more contentious by O'Connor's vacillating symbolic indicators.

Colors also seem to carry a symbolic implication for salvation in O'Connor's fictional representations, albeit once again, an unreliable one. Through her insistent allusions to hat and clothing colors, O'Connor prepares the reader for determining their significance as symbols. Inconsistencies in color symbolism, however, parallel O'Connor's inconsistencies with her hat symbols. Black and gray are colors commonly used to express somber or evil happenings, but as dark colors would also possess the property of heat absorption. O'Connor frequently seems to use these two colors as illustrations of corruption and sin, but she does not use this pattern exclusively. Very often black and gray, as colors, act in her fiction as sponge-absorbing pigments soaking up the sun's brilliant rays and as such would capture God's goodness. Which meaning does O'Connor intend for the colors black and gray? Her use of these colors appears to support both interpretations. Dark colors are sometimes impenetrable shields providing a second defense (the clothing itself being the first) against the infiltration of grace into the souls of the unsaved; in other instances they seem actually to extract the warmth of the sun transmitting it as God's grace into the immortal souls of those in possession of these symbolic colors.

As previously noted in "A Good Man Is Hard to Find," The Misfit and Hiram murder the grandmother and her family while wearing their black or gray hats, and the color itself is most certainly equated with evil at the moment of their sinning. Black also figures prominently in "The

Partridge Festival." Singleton, the mad murderer who shoots six townspeople in this story is visited by Calhoun and Mary Elizabeth in Quincy State Hospital. He is wearing a hospital gown, black shoes, and "On his head was a black hat, not the kind countrymen wear, but a black derby hat such as might be worn by a gunman in the movies" (*CS* 442). The reader comparing The Misfit, Hiram, and Singleton see characters shielded from the sun by their hats. In fact they are twice protected because the hats are black, or shades of black that O'Connor herself equated with movie gangsters. Lest the reader feel comfortable, however, that here is a recognizable and consistent symbolic indicator of evil in O'Connor's fiction, O'Connor's comments extolling The Misfit as a potential prophet, and Singleton as a devil dispel this myth (*MM* 113; *Collected* 1151). She writes to John Hawkes about both of these characters:

> About that grandmother and the Misfit: it is the fact that the old lady's gesture is the result of grace that makes it right that the Misfit shoot her. Grace is never received warmly. Always a recoil, or so I think. . . . and like you, I am all for Singleton in this, devil though I rightly consider him to be. He's one of those devils who go about piercing pretensions, not the devil who goes about like a roaring lion seeking whom he may devour. There is a hierarchy of devils surely. (*Collected* 1150-51)

Astonishingly, The Misfit's murder of six family members somehow differs in O'Connor's mind from the six murders committed by Singleton. Yet she associates the same black clothing symbolism with each of them.

Mrs. McIntyre from "The Displaced Person"

> had on a heavy black coat and a red head-kerchief with her black hat pulled down on top of it to keep the glare out of her eyes. Under the black brim her face had an abstracted look and once or twice her lips moved silently. (*CS* 234)

The intrusion of red in Mrs. McIntyre's description does not negate the use of the color black as an indicator of redemption. It is true that red in O'Connor does represent the blood of Christ. She has made this explicit in the final sentence of "A Temple of the Holy Ghost" when she compares the red ball of the sun to "an elevated Host drenched in blood" (*CS* 248). However, black still dominates in Mrs. McIntyre's description and in her fate, for with her black hat pulled over the red bandanna she completely covers any Christ connection and, therefore, effectively neutralizes any alliance with God. By allowing black to dominate and by utilizing the black brim as a double safeguard against admitting the glare of grace into her soul, O'Connor seems to take no chances with Mrs. McIntyre's spiritual fate. Adorned in black, Mrs. McIntyre watches as the tractor runs over Mr. Guizac's body.

Marshall Bruce Gentry sees Mrs. McIntyre as unsaved. He indicates that "There is some question about whether she receives grace at the end of her story after consenting to the killing of Mr. Guizac."[6] The question perhaps, emerges in part because of O'Connor's use of black as an indicator of evil. If the symbolism holds true, Mrs. McIntyre, dressed in black, should be damned. But O'Connor views Mrs. McIntyre as saved. In a November 1955 letter explaining the story to "A," she writes:

> The displaced person did accomplish a kind of redemption in that he destroyed the place, which was evil, and set Mrs. McIntyre on the road to a new kind of suffering, not Purgatory as St. Catherine would conceive it (realization) but Purgatory at least as a beginning of suffering. . . . Isn't her position, entirely helpless to herself, very like that of the souls in Purgatory? I missed making this clear but how are you going to make such things clear to people who don't believe in God, much less in Purgatory? (*HB* 118)

Purgatory, in Catholic belief, is a "place or condition of temporal punishment for those who, having died, are in venial sin or have not satisfied God's justice for mortal sins already forgiven."[7] Unlike banishment to Hell, which results in everlasting punishment by damning souls irrevocably stained by mortal sin to an eternal existence deprived of the sight of God, detainment in Purgatory means salvation is attainable for those souls that have repented of their wrongdoings before death. If Mrs. McIntyre is only destined for Purgatory, according to Catholic theology she is redeemable. Inasmuch as she, like Singleton and The Misfit, wears black, the color cannot be an accurate indicator of her spiritual fate.

Haze Motes in *Wise Blood* begins his journey with "a stiff black broad-brimmed hat on his lap, a hat that an elderly country preacher

---

[6]Gentry, *Flannery O'Connor's Religion of the Grotesque*, 103.

[7]John Deedy, *The Catholic Fact Book* (Chicago: Thomas More Press, 1986) 374.

would wear" (*Collected* 3). By the time he is ready to begin engaging in sin with Leora Watts, O'Connor describes him as having a face that "was stern and determined under the heavy hat" (*Collected* 15). When Haze preaches about the Church Without Christ, O'Connor bestows upon him a white hat (*Collected* 87). He still needs his hat as a weapon against the infiltration of grace, for although he preaches to any who will listen that "You needn't to look at the sky because it's not going to open up and show no place behind it," Haze is really terrified that the sky may very well open up to the rays of grace, and he must be outfitted with a hat to be shielded (*Collected* 93).

When Haze uses his car to run over and kill Solace Layfield, his look-alike is wearing a white hat and the implication is that Haze wears a white hat also since O'Connor makes reference to the "resemblance in their clothes" (*Collected* 114). Yet if O'Connor's symbolism were consistent, Haze's act of murder should call for him to don a black hat like The Misfit's or Singleton's. As *Wise Blood* continues, Haze, in an effort to pay for his crime of murder and for his life of disbelief, blinds himself. At this point in the story he is described as wearing a "wheat-colored" panama hat (*Collected* 128). As the story ends, however, when Haze is found dying in a ditch, the two policemen who find him make reference to his blue suit, but not to a hat.

Haze Motes's changing hat colors would seem to parallel the progression of his soul: black when he refuses God's grace and is at that point in the story, unsaved; white, which usually indicates purity and light when he kills Solace Layfield whose "death can be accepted as the end of Motes's double or false self"[8] and which symbolically represents the killing of his own evil inclinations; and finally wheat-colored, the color of the bread of life, when he punishes himself for uncleanliness and becomes in O'Connor's mind "a kind of saint" (*Collected* 941). It seems illogical to consider that O'Connor would not have meant colors as symbolic indicators when she makes an obvious attempt at including color in her vivid descriptions of her characters, and when we once again remember O'Connor's previously cited mandate to choose "every detail for a reason." But curiously, despite the fact that throughout the novel O'Connor makes continuous references to Haze's hats and their colors,

[8]Edward Kessler, *Flannery O'Connor and the Language of the Apocalypse* (Princeton: Princeton University Press, 1986) 122.

when Haze is found dying by the policemen, O'Connor makes no effort to indicate whether he possesses a hat of any color. The reader, who reasonably can assume from O'Connor's build-up that both hats and their colors support symbolic significance, is left confused as to what symbolic meaning is purposed.

O'Connor frequently uses physical afflictions as symbols of a character's limitations; she especially emphasizes eye problems. "As an instrument of perception, the eye is the source of light, intelligence, and spirit. It is also the window of the soul."[9] O'Connor's characters, through their visual afflictions, suffer additional restrictions in their quest toward salvation. Most wear glasses, some are blind or blind themselves, and some have their sight otherwise obstructed, as does Mrs. May in "Greenleaf" who is described as having "pale near-sighted eyes" and who first views the bull through venetian blinds (*CS* 313). O'Connor creates these handicaps as another attempt to symbolize the barriers her fictional characters have chosen (or that she, as author, has determined) that prevent their eyes (the symbol O'Connor has chosen for their souls) from being barraged with incoming rays of sunlight containing the saving grace of God.

O'Connor emphasizes her focus on vision in *Mystery and Manners*:

> For the writer of fiction, everything has its testing point in the eye, and the eye is an organ that eventually involves the whole personality, and as much of the world as can be got into it. It involves judgment. Judgment is something that begins in the act of vision, and when it does not, or when it becomes separated from vision, then a confusion exists in the mind which transfers itself to the story. (*MM* 91)

By creating a simple chart we can see how O'Connor works at creating a confusion that transfers itself to the minds of her readers as they attempt to decipher the code contained in her symbolic treatment of eyeglasses.

---

[9]Bettina L. Knapp, *Machine, Metaphor, and the Writer: A Jungian View* (University Park PA: Pennsylvania State University Press, 1989) 115.

CHARACTER	WEARS GLASSES WHEN SINNING	REMOVES GLASSES AFTER/DURING SINNING	POSSESSES GLASSES AT STORY'S END	POTENTIAL FOR GRACE (AS SEEN BY O'CONNOR)
The Misfit	Yes	Yes	Yes	Yes
Mary Fortune	Yes	Yes	No	Yes
Mr. Fortune	Yes	No (knocked off; tried to retain them)	No	No
Hulga	Yes	Yes (taken from her)	No	Yes
Bible salesman	No	Yes (Hulga's)	Yes	No

We glean from O'Connor's portrayal of The Misfit that his lack of visual acuity becomes symbolically more than just his lack of judgment in spiritual and moral matters when we examine the circumstances that surround him with and without his eyeglasses. His glasses act as an obstruction repelling God's light away from his eyes and thus from penetrating his soul. Glasses, generally considered to be devices used to aid poor vision or correct eye problems, take on the opposite meaning for O'Connor who wants us to consider them as physical barriers. She deliberately places them on the eyes of The Misfit when he kills the grandmother, but she indicates that he "put his gun down on the ground and took off his glasses and began to clean them" after the murder (*CS* 132). O'Connor seems, in this story, to have chosen this unusual symbolic barrier to deflect the sunshine of God's grace causing The Misfit to be unable or unwilling to arrive at proper spiritual decisions while wearing them.

When The Misfit's eyes are viewed without his glasses they seem to reflect his potentiality for grace upon which O'Connor is insistent. She describes him thus: "Without his glasses, The Misfit's eyes were red-rimmed and pale and defenseless-looking" (*CS* 132-33). This defenselessness is only apparent when his glasses are removed but seems to be the core around which O'Connor structures her rationalizations about the state of his eternal soul:

> I don't want to equate the Misfit with the devil. I prefer to think that, however unlikely this may seem, the old lady's gesture, like the mustard-seed, will grow to be a great crow-filled tree in the Misfit's heart, and will be enough of a pain to him there to turn him into the prophet he was meant to become. But that's another story. (*MM* 112-13)

After The Misfit shoots the grandmother, O'Connor makes him aware on some level that he has denied God, and she alerts her readers to this fact by momentarily allowing him to remove and attempt to cleanse this barrier. The act of removing this physical barrier and O'Connor's use of the verbal construction "began to clean" reinforce the idea that she intended his eyeglasses as symbolic impediments and they are, perhaps, the vehicle through which O'Connor's attempts to portray the state of The Misfit's soul. She makes a parenthetical time reference to The Misfit's moment of grace in a 14 April 1960 letter to John Hawkes that bears mention:

> His shooting [of the grandmother] is a recoil, a horror at her humanness, but after he has done it and cleaned his glasses, the Grace has worked in him and he pronounces his judgment: she would have been a good woman if *he* had been there every moment of her life. (*Collected* 1125)

The Misfit's grace seems only available "after" he was able to remove and clean the symbolic eyeglass barrier. The story ends with no further mention of The Misfit's glasses, though the reader would expect that they are still in his possession. We might assume from this story that it is the wearing of glasses (not their possession) that prohibits the intake of grace.

The very title of "A View of the Woods" invites a reliance on vision as symbol. It is significant, however, that Mr. Fortune, whom O'Connor indicates as damned, can only *view* the woods O'Connor delineates as "pure enough to be a Christ symbol if anything is" (*HB* 190). Throughout the story, O'Connor makes constant comparisons of Mary Fortune Pitts and Mr. Fortune indicating their similarities:

> her face—a small replica of the old man's—
>
> she was like him on the inside too.
>
> the spiritual distance between them was slight.

> He liked to think of her as being thoroughly of his clay.
>
> Her glasses were silver-rimmed like his and she even walked the way he did . . . (*CS* 336; 336; 336; 338; 339)

Both Mary Fortune and Mr. Fortune do wear glasses, but O'Connor makes several references to Mary Fortune's eyes, which seem to put her in a category similar to The Misfit's:

> Her pale eyes behind her spectacles followed the repeated motion . . .
>
> Her eyes were puffy and pink-rimmed . . . (*CS* 335; 347)

O'Connor does believe that Mary Fortune, like The Misfit, is saved. She wrote to "A" on 28 December 1956:

> Part of the tension of the story is created by Mary Fortune and the old man being images of each other but opposite in the end. One is saved and the other is dammed [sic], and there is no way out of it, it must be pointed out and underlined. Their fates are different. (*Collected* 1015)

Mary Fortune Pitts, in her deadly battle with her grandfather, tells him to take off his glasses. Mary Fortune's order to her grandfather as they begin their fight to the death could be seen symbolically as her last attempt to help him see God through uncovered eyes. She removes her glasses, but Mr. Fortune will not. In the intensity of their struggle, Mr. Fortune's glasses are knocked off. How does the symbolic barrier of eyeglasses in this story conform with its use in "A Good Man Is Hard to Find"? Mary Fortune, who is saved in O'Connor's estimation, does wear glasses when she is behaving like her grandfather, but removes them when she fights against him, a fight precipitated by his determination to destroy the woods, the Christ symbol. Her eyes at the moment of her death are unshielded, so she, like The Misfit, can be saved. Her grandfather, a man spiritually condemned according to O'Connor, also dies without his glasses, although being without them was truly not of his own volition. While he is left at the moment of death without his glasses, Mr. Fortune had actively sought to retain them, an authorial decision that seems consistent with O'Connor's intention to refuse him grace, but inconsistent with the overall symbolic treatment of glasses used to encircle either Mary Fortune or The Misfit (see chart p. 45). If O'Connor intended symbolic consistency, shouldn't Mr. Fortune have died with his glasses on? Additionally neither Mary Fortune nor Mr. Fortune possesses glasses at the end of the story; The Misfit (who like Mary Fortune is considered saved) was still in possession of his. One must wonder at least, why the symbolism surrounding Mary Fortune, which had been so like that surrounding The Misfit, differs in this respect if both are redeemable.

Sally Fitzgerald, in a footnote to one of O'Connor's letters to "A" in 1956, discusses the transformation that would have occurred in the destinies of Mr. Fortune and his granddaughter if O'Connor had not deleted the following paragraph:

> Pitts, by accident, found them that evening. He was walking home through the woods about sunset. The rain had stopped but the polished trees were hung with clear drops of water that turned red where the sun touched them; the air was saturated with dampness. He came on them suddenly and shied backward, his foot not a yard from where they lay. For almost a minute he stood still and then, his knees buckling, he squatted down by their sides and stared into their eyes, in the pale blue pools of rainwater that the sky had filled. (*HB* 190)

In this ending the eyes of Mr. Fortune and his granddaughter are filled with the pale blue reflective water of God's saving grace. As Fitzgerald notes: "The paragraph she omitted seems to suggest that although both were doomed, having destroyed each other, in the end both had their eyes opened and filled with rain, even possibly with tears."[10] This paragraph does indicate the emphasis O'Connor places on the eyes of her characters. Eyes unshielded are obviously intended as the pathway to the soul through which God's grace may flow. Interestingly enough, O'Connor chose to end this story without this paragraph. She wanted only Mary Fortune to be available for grace. But Mr. Fortune, like his granddaughter, also dies without his glasses; why, then, can't he see?

If we make an attempt to reconcile O'Connor's symbolic treatment of Mr. Fortune, Mary Fortune, and The Misfit with her assessments of their salvation (or potential salvation) as it relates to their connection with

[10]Sally Fitzgerald, editor, *The Habit of Being: Letters of Flannery O'Connor* (New York: Farrar, Straus, and Giroux, 1979) 190.

eyeglasses, we can almost defend a sort of consistency: Mr. Fortune, who refused to relinquish his visual barrier, is destined for eternal damnation; Mary Fortune Pitts, who removed her glasses in behavior that mimics The Misfit's, is symbolically permitted to enter the kingdom of heaven. At least that is the conclusion a reader might reach after reading "A Good Man Is Hard to Find" and "A View of the Woods." But what might the reader conclude about the symbolic intent of wearing, not wearing, possessing, or not possessing glasses after reading "Good Country People"?

In "Good Country People," Joy-Hulga wears glasses until the Bible salesman takes them off. If we can trust O'Connor's visual symbolism, Hulga's moment of grace comes at the end of the story for at that point her sight becomes unfettered and presumably she will be able to accept salvation. O'Connor believed the theft of Hulga's wooden leg would alert readers to the fact that the Bible salesman "has taken away part of the girl's personality and has revealed her deeper affliction to her for the first time" (*MM* 99). In terms of O'Connor's eyeglass symbolism, Hulga's revelation only comes after the Bible salesman seizes her glasses, just as The Misfit's eyes only become red-rimmed after he removes his glasses. Therefore, if the symbol of glasses is to remain constant, the Bible salesman, whose corruption endures, should be visually impaired as he violates Hulga. The Bible salesman, however, never wears eyeglasses. Instead, O'Connor pointedly puts him in possession of Hulga's glasses and "a woman's glass eye" (*CS* 291). Presumably Hulga's glasses could be perceived as clouding the Bible salesman's vision if he wore them, but they remain in his pocket. And a prosthesis not his own, the woman's glass eye, could hardly be viewed as interfering with his sight as it would be physically impossible for him to insert it, thus making it worthless to him as an optical impediment. These items remain useless to him as shields while he acts the devil, but both are items that he willfully seeks to possess.

The Bible salesman is never described as wearing glasses when he commits his sins and thus seems unlike The Misfit. Yet at the end of this story he, like The Misfit, is in possession of optical devices (see chart p. 45). If we know that O'Connor intended the Bible salesman as damned, we can accept this symbolic treatment as an indication that he has not accepted the unshielded posture that would make his eyes ready for a beatific vision. The quandary facing the reader becomes one of resolving the vacillating symbolic connotation of glasses as possible barriers to grace with O'Connor's own explanations of the redemptive potential for

The Misfit and the Bible salesman. Fluctuating symbolic patterns do seem to be authorial devices O'Connor employs to keep her "message from becoming transparent." But readers coming to the text assume dependability in symbolic meaning. When confronted with the abundant inconsistencies present in these stories, readers fall back on O'Connor's own explications if they are aware of them, or create their own varying interpretations if they are not. O'Connor's symbolic oscillations in this story heavily constrain a consistent, reliable interpretation of her use of eyeglasses.

In his discussion of "Greenleaf" in *The Pruning Word,* John R. May writes that "Mrs. May stands condemned." He emphasizes the evidence present in the text that yields this reading: Mrs. May's "freezing *unbelief,*" that she "*finds the light unbearable,*" and that she only "*seemed* . . . to be bent over whispering some last discovery into the animal's ear."[11] May's interpretation of Mrs. May's fate would seem to corroborate the validity of O'Connor's visual symbolism as an indication of redemption. Symbolically Mrs. May's damnation seems continually reinforced through the use of visual inferences. O'Connor has her close her eyes while she waits for Mr. Greenleaf.

> Through her closed eyes, she could feel the sun, red-hot overhead. She opened her eyes slightly but the white light forced her to close them again. (*CS* 332)

When Mrs. May is gored by the bull,

> She continued to stare straight ahead but the entire scene in front of her had changed—the tree line was a dark wound in a world that was nothing but sky . . . (*CS* 332)

Mrs. May is permitted to feel the sun. But even when she tries to open her eyes, they are "forced" closed by the brightness of God's message. She does seem to be rejected by God who constrains her from viewing the sun in the world O'Connor makes for her. O'Connor's visual symbolism does not always produce this same critical interpretation, however. David Eggenschwiler reads the ending of "Greenleaf" as

---

[11]John R. May, *The Pruning Word: the Parables of Flannery O'Connor* (Notre Dame: University of Notre Dame Press, 1976) 101. May's emphasis throughout.

"unmistakably a religious revelation" that results in the salvation of Mrs. May.[12] He sees Mrs. May as being "racked by an unendurable light of revelation and by a purifying love that must destroy the old self."[13] Does O'Connor mean for Mrs. May to be condemned as May believes? She has been denied the sun. Or does O'Connor make mention of the sky in Mrs. May's final world to indicate that her view of God is nigh, and she will soon be saved as Eggenschwiler theorizes? It is easy to see how such diametrically opposed critical assessments can be made of Mrs. May's fate. The reader, presented with conflicting messages within the story itself, struggles to grasp how O'Connor's God could destroy Mrs. May's old sinful self yet forcefully deny her a view of the light that could assure her deliverance from sin and welcome her entrance into heaven.

Eyes, eyesight, and vision are also important to the interpretation of "The Displaced Person." In this story, Mrs. McIntyre procures damnation for herself when both she and Mr. Shortley allow Mr. Guizac to be killed. O'Connor makes their eyes their spiritual barometers. Mrs. McIntyre's spiritual condemnation is signaled symbolically when O'Connor writes:

> She had felt her eyes and Mr. Shortley's eyes and the Negro's eyes come together in one look that froze them in collusion forever, and she had heard the little noise the Pole made as the tractor wheel broke his backbone. (*CS* 234)

As she lays in bed, incapacitated by the realization of her participation in murder, Mrs. McIntyre is left apparently unable to repent. "Her eyesight grew steadily worse" (*CS* 235). O'Connor impedes her vision as she prepares her for death. For Mrs. McIntyre there is no moment of grace. Her eyes have participated in the crime; her soul is irrevocably stained, and O'Connor refuses her the final vision. Or so it might seem. But as indicated in the previous section on color symbolism, O'Connor only meant to detain Mrs. McIntyre in Purgatory. Can we trust O'Connor's symbols to be reliable indicators of salvation?

In O'Connor's two novels, Haze Motes and Tarwater present comparable portraits of developing prophets. Haze's visual difficulties, however, include a problem with his ancestry. In the beginning of *Wise*

---

[12]David Eggenschwiler, *The Christian Humanism of Flannery O'Connor* (Detroit: Wayne State University Press, 1972) 62.

[13]Ibid., 64.

Blood O'Connor mentions the "pair of silver-rimmed spectacles that had belonged to his mother," yet Haze, unlike O'Connor's short story protagonists, goes beyond possessing or putting on glasses to avoid the light of God *(Collected* 12). He deliberately and permanently destroys his sight toward the end of the novel. Haze's visual impediment in *Wise Blood* is the antithesis of that in O'Connor's short stories because Haze's self-blinding is carried out as an act of contrition causing him to develop into "a kind of Protestant saint" (*Collected* 923); "his blindness becomes a life-in-death symbol" (*MM* 72). O'Connor writes that "When Haze blinds himself he turns entirely to an inner vision" (*Collected* 921). Haze also meets O'Connor's most stringent criterion for redemption: "Either one is serious about salvation or one is not" (*MM* 167). Haze is serious. The treatment of his lack of vision in this novel, however, adds confusion to O'Connor's handling of visual problems in her short stories.

In O'Connor's second novel, Tarwater, after he has drowned Bishop but before he is raped, wishes that the sun would "get out of the sky altogether or to be veiled in a cloud. He turned his face enough to rid his vision of it" (*Collected* 465). After his violation has occurred O'Connor writes that "His eyes looked small and seedlike as if while he was asleep, they had been lifted out, scorched, and dropped back into his head" (*Collected* 472). His eyes have received the seeds of grace. O'Connor ends this novel with the following paragraph:

> He stood clenching the blackened burnt-out pine bough. Then after a moment he began to move forward again slowly. He knew that he could not turn back now. He knew that his destiny forced him on to a final revelation. His scorched eyes no longer looked hollow or as if they were meant only to guide him forward. They looked as if, touched with a coal like the lips of the prophet, they would never be used for ordinary sights again. (*Collected* 473)

The action of God through the fire-scorching of Tarwater's eyes earns him his redemptive standing in O'Connor's fiction; his vision now can become Vision. Until Tarwater accepted this grace of God forced upon him, his eyes did not see. Tarwater, like Haze Motes, comes through violence to realize his mission as prophet. But unlike Haze, he need not be blind to receive his inner sight. O'Connor's treatment of the sun, eyes, and vision remains inconsistent throughout her fictional works.

In his article "The Mechanical in *Everything That Rises Must Converge*," Jeffrey J. Folks writes:

> the mechanical plays a key role in O'Connor's comic aesthetic. The machine is not just a neutral force to be controlled by humane purposes —it is the best representative symbol for the repetitive, mechanical element in which human beings live most of the time.[14]

Folks ends his article by asserting that "O'Connor's realism is the aesthetic foundation for a comic art in which the concrete details of mechanization are the source of her greatest humor."[15] In O'Connor's fiction, however, the machine does little to contribute to humor. Use of the mechanical for O'Connor is also not a sign representing a humdrum existence, nor is it a neutral force to be controlled for human purposes. Rather, in O'Connor's works, the machine represents the reliance on science by humanity which caused movement away from an earlier age when the sensibilities demanded complete faith and trust in God.

Repeatedly, in O'Connor's fiction, the machine appears in the form of cars, trucks, and trains to serve as symbols delineating the salvation of the characters who are intimately associated with them. O'Connor explains Haze's Essex in *Mystery and Manners*:

> To take an example from my own book, *Wise Blood*, the hero's rat-colored automobile is his pulpit and his coffin as well as something he thinks of as a means of escape. He is mistaken in thinking that it is a means of escape, of course, and does not really escape his predicament until the car is destroyed by the patrolman. The car is a kind of death-in-life symbol, as his blindness is a life-in-death symbol. The fact that these meanings are there makes the book significant. The reader may not see them but they have their effect on him nonetheless. This is the way the modern novelist sinks, or hides, his theme. (*MM* 72)

While in possession of his Essex, Haze is not able to realize his mission. Not until the "death-in-life symbol" is destroyed, can either Haze or Tarwater elude their difficulties. For Tarwater, too, remains unable to answer his calling until he is thrown from the car by the stranger who

---

[14]Jeffrey J. Folks, "The Mechanical in *Everything That Rises Must Converge*," in *The Southern Literary Journal* 18/2 (Spring 1986): 25.

[15]Ibid.

rapes him. Only then can he symbolically escape his tie to evil. The novel ends with him walking toward the city to begin his mission of prophecy.

Mr. Fortune, who kills his granddaughter, begins and ends his fictional existence associated with machinery. When "A View of the Woods" opens, he and his granddaughter sit in his parked car watching the construction machines clear the woods from the land he has sold. As the story ends "He looked around desperately for someone to help him but the place was deserted except for one huge yellow monster which sat to the side, as stationary as he was, gorging itself on clay" (*CS* 356). O'Connor, in discussing this story with "A" in December of 1956, wrote: "Some prediction of hell for the old man is essential to my story" (*Collected* 1011). She was firm in her insistence that the woods are "the Christ symbol" indicating that they "walk across the water, they are bathed in a red light, and they in the end escape the old man's vision and march off over the hills" (*Collected* 1014). O'Connor has damned the old man and has symbolized this by intimately linking him with both cars and construction machinery.

If we use the machinery symbolism in her two novels and this story as guides to interpretation, characters who remain with their machines, or maintain a connection with their machines should not achieve redemption. But as we have already seen, the disposition of Mrs. McIntyre's soul is not clearly indicated despite her connection with machinery. Mrs. McIntyre stands by while the tractor runs over Mr. Guizac. Is she symbolically condemned to hell on earth unable to silence the priest who preaches Catholic doctrine to her unwilling soul? O'Connor does not think so. Additionally, Mrs. May has just reached inside her car to honk the horn for Mr. Greenleaf when she is gored to death. Critical explications vary with respect to Mrs. May's salvation or lack thereof, but she, too, has an association with machinery. Does she find "the light [of God] unbearable" because she stands condemned (*CS* 333)? Reading the machinery symbol in the manner suggested by the two novels would indicate an affirmation. But this O'Connor symbol, like the others, is not reliable.

In a discussion of O'Connor's portrayal of Christ in her fiction, Orvell writes that "sometimes an image of divine intervention would have no human shape at all: the 'Greenleaf' bull, the icicled bird of 'The

Enduring Chill,' the tattoo on 'Parker's Back.'"[16] What Orvell calls "an image of divine intervention" actually operates on a symbolic level for O'Connor. O'Connor is adept at transforming the ordinary into the extraordinary, but this masterful manipulation carries with it some risks. The reader's difficulties with O'Connor's symbolic choices parallel the difficulties found with her linguistic choices. In both cases O'Connor's forced meanings define commonplace objects or language in atypical ways. Readers who bring to her text a grasp of traditionally recognizable symbols that are part of the Christian belief system find distractions in the symbolic strangeness that runs counter to conventional Catholic expectations.

In his examination of the bull in "Greenleaf," Eggenschwiler explains that O'Connor

> often uses satanic instruments to enlighten her characters: she is not only showing that God moves in mysterious ways and brings good out of evil; she is also exploring the psychological and religious view that demonic characters experience God's mercy through demonic structures that oppose or caricature their own forms of idolatry.[17]

The "Greenleaf" bull, which May terms her "most effective use of natural symbolism," from the beginning of the story is overtly designated as God's representative on earth.[18] O'Connor begins and ends this story with sentences referencing the bull as unmistakably a Christ symbol; he is structurally created as the alpha and omega, the omnipresent god-figure. From the very first the bull is compared to a "patient god come down to woo her" (*CS* 311). His adornment with a crown of thorns in the first paragraph leaves little doubt that O'Connor was drawing large figures for her blind audience. By the end of the story Mrs. May meets her fate; she has been wooed by her "wild tormented lover," stabbed in the heart by one of his horns, and held fast "in an unbreakable grip" to become, however unwilling, the bride of Christ: behaviors and actions all counter to the traditional Catholic expectations of Christ as loving bridegroom.

---

[16]Miles Orvell, *Invisible Parade: The Fiction of Flannery O'Connor* (Philadelphia: Temple University Press, 1972) 40.

[17]Eggenschwiler, *The Christian Humanism of Flannery O'Connor*, 64.

[18]May, *The Pruning Word*, 98.

Eggenschwiler is correct; O'Connor's God does move in mysterious ways. Hopefully, her heaven includes a support group for battered wives.

In discussing her story "The Enduring Chill" with Caroline Gordon Tate, O'Connor writes: "I'm busy with The Holy Ghost. He is going to be a waterstain—very obvious but the only thing possible" (*Collected* 1054). Throughout the story, O'Connor mentions the waterstained ceiling in Asbury's bedroom. All references describe it as "a fierce bird" and connect it with ice imagery. She writes about Asbury's moment of grace to Ted R. Spivey:

> it's the knowlege [sic] that he has no high and tragic mortal illness but only a cow's disease that brings the shock of self-knowlege [sic] that clears the way for the Holy Ghost. (*Collected* 1076)

But O'Connor's Catholic audience is more accustomed to considering the Holy Ghost (or Holy Spirit, the name used more commonly after Vatican Council II) in the form of a dove. As John Deedy writes, the dove "is the symbol of the Holy Spirit, perhaps because of its gentleness and purity of appearance."[19] And F. J. Sheed explains that the Holy Spirit, the third person of the Trinity "is the utterance of the love of Father and Son" in Catholic theology.[20] The Holy Spirit is also depicted as a tongue of flame which visited the disciples on Pentecost to infuse them with the spirit of God. Faithful Catholics receive the Holy Spirit in the Sacrament of Confirmation as the special grace that will enable them to profess their faith as soldiers of Christ. O'Connor's bird, with a stabbing icicle in its beak brings no message of love, nor the strength to be part of God's army. Instead, O'Connor's description of it as a "fierce bird" who would descend "emblazoned in ice instead of fire" to impart an enduring chill causing "purifying terror" embodies it with monstrous and horrifying proportions (*CS* 382). O'Connor has radically departed from the common theological interpretations accepted by the faithful Catholic congregation of both her day and of the present to create a symbol of fear, not one of love or strength.

Geoffrey N. Leech and Michael H. Short in *Style in Fiction* discuss symbolism in literature:

---

[19]Deedy, *The Catholic Fact Book*, 338.

[20]F. J. Sheed, *Theology for Beginners* (Ann Arbor: Servant Books, 1981) 37.

> In very general terms, criteria of artistic relevance are of two apparently opposed kinds, summed up in the Aristotelian notion that it is the function of literature to express the universal through the particular. On the one hand, there is the impulse to specify such details, in the mock reality, as can be interpreted as standing for something beyond themselves, something universally important in the human condition. In this sense, the message itself, in literature, becomes a code, a symbolic structure.[21]

To consider message as symbol in O'Connor's fiction establishes a major stumbling block to readers determined to locate the Catholic theme O'Connor insists is present in all of her works. O'Connor's message relies heavily on the teachings of St. Augustine wherein lies the root of "misreadings" by a modern audience. Jay P. Dolan details the philosophy of St. Augustine:

> The Augustinian tradition espoused a very pessimistic concept of the human being. Original sin had undermined the strength of men and women and made them victims of sin. Gifted with freedom but bewitched by sin, men and women had to struggle to attain holiness on earth and salvation afterward. In some religious traditions, the Calvinist being the most notable, salvation was reserved for a chosen few, the elect of God. For others, Catholics among them, holiness and salvation was open to all, but you had to earn it; the way you did this was through a victorious struggle over sin. Since humanity was so inclined to evil, however, people needed a great deal of assistance in their battle against sin.[22]

O'Connor certainly adhered to belief in the depravity of the human condition. Her fictional presentation of a world tainted, nay contaminated, by original sin falls squarely into an Augustinian belief system. But O'Connor's fictional message goes beyond St. Augustine's theology when her characters are symbolically restrained from partaking in the battle. By enforcing a symbolic system which thwarts the ability to receive grace by some of her characters she enters into an almost Calvinistic interpretation of an elect. And while she has provided a "moment of grace" to assist

---

[21]Leech and Short, *Style in Fiction*, 155.

[22]Jay P. Dolan, *The American Catholic Experience: A History from Colonial Times to the Present* (New York: Doubleday & Company, Inc., 1985) 226.

some characters to achieve their ultimate salvation, not all of her characters are privy to this gift. In fact, through the creation of symbols such as her sunshading hats, visual barriers, and machine symbolism, O'Connor has removed from some of the characters who are associated with them redemption as a viable option. Salvation is not open to all.

The reasons for O'Connor's critical misinterpretations are best summarized by Frederick Crews in the following statement:

> For all of her private loyalty to the Church's hopeful teachings, then, the world of O'Connor's fiction remains radically askew. Readers immersed in that fiction without a lifeline to the doctrinal assurance found in her lectures and letters tend to feel an existential vertigo at the very moments where the Christian critics want them to feel most worshipful. And this response cannot be dismissed as a mere error, a product of incomplete knowledge. O'Connor's works, we must understand, are not finally about salvation but about doom—the sudden and irremediable realization that there is no exit from being, for better or worse, exactly who one is.[23]

Whether O'Connor meant to deny grace to all but the chosen is moot; the implication derived from her symbols is not. Her unorthodox treatment of common symbols as barriers and impediments to receiving salvation cause her language to escape her stated theology. In her fiction there is the "elect of God" and there is the damned, and determining which is which often becomes an insurmountable task in part because of the erratic nature of her symbols and her uniquely idiosyncratic linguistic system.

[23]Crews, "The Power of Flannery O'Connor," 55.

3.
Images Versus Religious Intent in O'Connor's Fiction

The Heath Guide to Literature describes an image as "a group of words that records sense impressions directly."[1] Other basic literature anthologies commonly describe images as word-pictures. O'Connor's talent as an artist resides in her ability to make the reader see in great detail her fictional world. O'Connor relies heavily on imagery as a telescopic device permitting a glimpse into her deeply embedded religious message. Although discovery of O'Connor's religious objectives are possible through an analysis of her images, the images O'Connor presents often seem to run counter to traditional Catholic conceptions.

Wesley Kort writes that in the creation of any narrative, "The discipline becomes a process in which images of the artist and the reader are created and brought together."[2] But O'Connor's imagery does little to effect such a union. Her application of imagery merges with her use of symbol, language, and metaphor to produce a fictional product whose eccentricity yields instead, readers who often "read" interpretations radically opposed to those she as author apparently intended. Roger Fowler's explanation of the intricacies of language interpretation helps to explain why this might be so:

> Language is a powerfully committing medium to work in. It does not allow us to 'say something' without conveying an attitude to that something. When we speak or write, the words and sentences we choose resonate for our hearers and and [sic] readers, emitting potential significance which are only partly under our control.[3]

O'Connor's imagery, therefore, says something about her private views of religious doctrine which may not always have been intentionally conveyed. Her images, like her language and symbols, assume existences

---

[1]David Bergman and Daniel Mark Epstein, *The Heath Guide to Literature* (Lexington MA: D. C. Heath and Company, 1984) 555.

[2]Wesley A. Kort, *Narrative Elements and Religious Meaning* (Philadelphia: Fortress Press, 1975) 5.

[3]Roger Fowler, *Linguistics and the Novel* (London: Methuen & Co. Ltd., 1977) 76.

of their own, wrestling control away from her personal Catholic convictions which appear quite traditional in her private correspondence.

O'Connor writes that the fiction writer is

> looking for one image that will connect or combine or embody two points; one is a point in the concrete, and the other is a point not visible to the naked eye, but believed in by him firmly, just as real to him, really, as the one that everybody sees. (*MM* 42)

The problem in interpreting O'Connor's fictional images as representational of her religious intent to educate her reading public to an awareness of the God she believed they abandoned, is that her vision is not "the one that everybody sees." And for this reason, Fowler's analysis of what actually occurs when a reader assesses an author's linguistic choices must be considered when the reader examines O'Connor's image patterns. Fowler writes:

> Selecting the linguistic structures that are available to him for his work of representation, the novelist loses some degree of personal control—the culture's values (including expectations about types of implied author) seep through, infiltrate his utterance, so that personal expression is necessarily qualified by the social meanings which attach to the expressions he chooses.[4]

Fowler also states that "Language, transcending the individual, imprints the text with the community's values."[5] Yet shared community values become the very dilemma that confounds a traditionally Catholic perception of O'Connor. While she wanted to reach her contemporaries whom she thought had assisted in begetting a world in which "the vaporization of religion" had occurred in order to convince them of their spiritual delinquency, O'Connor's methods obstruct such an interpretation (*MM* 161). Her images orchestrate, instead, hindrances that impede an accurate assessment of her intended message.

In an attempt to reach a nation of readers who have abandoned religion, O'Connor believed that:

---

[4]Ibid, 80.

[5]Ibid.

> The novelist doesn't write to express himself, he doesn't write simply to render a vision he believes true, rather he renders his vision so that it can be transferred, as nearly whole as possible, to his reader. You can safely ignore the reader's taste, but you can't ignore his nature, you can't ignore his limited patience. Your problem is going to be difficult in direct proportion as your beliefs depart from his. (*MM* 162)

In order to transfer her vision to this problematic reader, O'Connor uses techniques such as distortion and exaggeration for she feels that

> Distortion . . . is an instrument; exaggeration has a purpose. . . . This is not the kind of distortion that destroys; it is the kind that reveals, or should reveal. (*MM* 162)

But O'Connor's distortions, for many readers, position her outside any shared recognizable Catholic culture and outside any general understanding readers might have of Catholic belief. Her images, which remain foreign to the cultural values of the shared Catholic imagination, like her style and symbols, become instead antithetical in meaning for the majority of the Catholic and Christian cultural community. Her treatment of the unusual not only reveals the "distortion that destroys" but seems, moreover, to focus insistently on those destructive forces for an audience perhaps more traditionally Christian in its imagination than she assumed.

In developing her fictional imagery O'Connor often surpasses the "limited patience" of a reading public guided to conclusions she most probably did not intend. Hawkes's view supports this assumption:

> My own feeling is that just as the creative process threatens the Holy throughout Flannery O'Connor's fiction by generating a paradoxical fusion of improbability and passion out of the Protestant "do-it-yourself" evangelism of the South, and thereby raises the pitch of apocalyptic experience when it finally appears; so too, throughout this fiction, the creative process transforms the writer's objective Catholic knowledge of the devil into an authorial attitude in itself in some measure diabolical.[6]

---

[6]John Hawkes, "Flannery O'Connor's Devil," *Sewanee Review* 70/3 (July-September 1962): 13.

O'Connor's world is peopled with her autocratic images of disharmony in family relationships, animalistic portraits of humanity, blasphemous and sacrilegious portrayals, and inanimate images that deny spirituality to God's chosen. Her grim vision of both God and his chosen deny the good news in the gospel. The peculiar imagery she so generously intersperses throughout her fiction complements her linguistic and symbolic choices which diverge from her expressed orthodox Catholic beliefs and depart radically from the beliefs of her audience.

O'Connor believed that

> When fiction is made according to its nature, it should reinforce our sense of the supernatural by grounding it in concrete, observable reality. (*MM* 148)

Throughout her writing, O'Connor makes an attempt to enlighten her audience to the preeminence of supernatural elements in the ordinary world, or as she stated to "the presence of grace as it appears in nature" (*MM* 147). In "You Can't Be Any Poorer Than Dead," the short story that became the nucleus for O'Connor's second novel, Tarwater notices that the

> Clouds were moving convulsively across a black sky and there was a pink unsteady moon that appeared to be jerked up a foot or so and then dropped and jerked up again. This was because, as he observed in an instant, the sky was lowering, coming down fast to smother him. (*CS* 308)

In this passage O'Connor deftly scatters her landscape with indications of celestial power: clouds, sky, moon. However, these divine images are combined with threatening concepts embodied in the lexicon O'Connor chooses. "Convulsively," "unsteady," "jerked," and "smother" are word choices that obliterate the intimation of the "good" implied in the Christian word "salvation" and forge together to convey fearful expectations of a raging and violent God, the God O'Connor feels is necessary to jar humanity into spiritual awareness, but a God more reminiscent of the retributional God of the Old Testament who might be unwelcomed by many of the faithful flock.

The landscape images O'Connor uses in "A Good Man Is Hard to Find" make use of constant impressions that reinforce the living presence of God the Redeemer as an omnipresent being in a disbelieving world.

As the grandmother's family begins their fateful trip, O'Connor makes reference to "Stone Mountain" and the "blue granite" along the highway, references that serve as images associated with the rock rolled in front of Christ's tomb, as well as being referential images suggesting Peter, the rock upon whom the Catholic Church was built. God is available in this world to those who can see. Trees and wood, their by-product, are omnipresent in the grandmother's world as a reminder of the reality of the wooden cross of Christ's suffering and his redemption for all his earthly creatures. The light becomes sun, or Son, and the colors red, purple, and blue, replete in O'Connor's natural surroundings, emerge in her fictional environments to serve presumably as an indication of the Georgia landscape as well as an indication of God's majestic presence in the land of the lost. These images, which are as real in O'Connor's world as she feels they should become in the lives of her readers, layer upon nature's earthly occurrences the spiritual propinquity of Christ the King to his earth-bound creations. However, O'Connor's linguistic choices determined by her preference for a nominal style often obscure the divinity she means to suggest with these references. By burying Christ-suggesting images in subordinate positions in the sentence as either objects of a prepositional phrase or as adjectival modifiers, two characteristics that may often accompany a nominal style, O'Connor interferes with the accessibility of these images as religious signals for her reading public.[7]

In "A Good Man Is Hard to Find," O'Connor details the start of the family's journey. She writes that the grandmother

> pointed out interesting details of the scenery: Stone Mountain; the blue granite that in some places came up to both sides of the highway; the brilliant red clay banks slightly streaked with purple; and the various crops that made rows of green lace-work on the ground. The trees were full of silver-white sunlight and the meanest of them sparkled. (*CS* 119)

O'Connor's attempt to connect the natural with the supernatural is minimalized by her use of images that receive little impact structurally. The critical reader will observe that although O'Connor may expect that the images in this text will evoke associations with God and religion, the intended force is mitigated due to her choice of punctuation. The images

---

[7]For a discussion of O'Connor's nominal style, see chapter 1. Citation from Cluett, *Prose Style and Critical Reading*, 74.

that have religious implications—"Stone Mountain," "blue granite," "brilliant red clay banks," "purple," "crops," "green," "ground"—become subordinated after the colon, reducing them to mere listings as items of interest. Moreover, the deep structure of the second sentence of this passage becomes significant. For our purposes we will consider deep structure as does Roger Fowler, which he explains thus:

> the most important aspects of the deep structure of a sentence are *proposition* and *modality*. The propositional element of the deep structure of a sentence makes reference to some phenomenon or idea outside of language, and attributes some property to it. Thus
>
> The dog barks
>
> picks out, refers to, a category of objects in our extra-linguistic experience (dog) and predicates an action of it (barks). The relationship between the noun and the predicate forms the semantic skeleton of the proposition. . . .
>
> Modality covers all those features of discourse which concern a speaker's or writer's attitude to, or commitment to, the value or applicability of the propositional content of an utterance . . .[8]

O'Connor's sentence—"The trees were full of silver-white sunlight and the meanest of them sparkled"—becomes in its deep structure: "[The] trees were full; [the] meanest sparkled." The "silver-white sunlight," the potential indicator of God's grace, is lessened by its syntactic application as the object of the preposition "of." The adjective, "silver-white," serves only as a cursory descriptor of the all important noun "sunlight," dramatically lessening its dynamic. Given her religious proclivity, O'Connor was perhaps striving to alert the reader to the religious significance of the trees from which Christ's cross was made by associating it with God's brilliant light. But by burying the celestial connection as an adjective within the prepositional phrase that impacts upon the adjective "full," O'Connor deflects the focus away from the distinctive Christ image, hiding it in nonemphasis. The reader must remain especially attentive to merge O'Connor's images with her oft reaffirmed spiritual message, otherwise stylistically these images vanish silently into the text.

---

[8]Fowler, *Linguistics and the Novel*, 12-13.

The modality of this same sentence, explained by Fowler as that which "relates directly to point of view in fiction,"[9] also causes the reader some pause. Robert Fitzgerald in his introduction to *Everything That Rises Must Converge* states that the last sentence of the O'Connor passage above is representative of O'Connor's conception that both nature and her characters are capable of sparkling.[10] However, Fitzgerald attributes this sentence to "The Artificial Nigger." As his source is erroneous, (the sentence comes from "A Good Man Is Hard to Find") so is his assessment of O'Connor's imagery and its impact. The humanism Fitzgerald wishes O'Connor's reading public to see seems decidedly absent as the structure and modality of this imagery suggest. If the trees are to be seen by the reader as an image of Christ's suffering and, therefore, the pivotal point of the redemptive process, O'Connor's choice of the adjective "meanest" as the noun of this sentence diminishes any intended religious implication. The force of the utterance revolves around the nominalized adjective used in the subject position, and the adjective-noun chosen by O'Connor to carry the weight of the statement introduces an ambiguity in definition. Does O'Connor intend "meanest" to indicate "those of humble origin," or "the lowliest" who would also deserve salvation, or does she envision this word as connoting "maliciousness" which thus becomes a commentary on the cruelty controlling her world?

To explore this concept of concealed religious images further we can extract the words that function as nouns/pronouns in O'Connor's description of the scenery in this same excerpt. They are:

> Mountain, granite, that [relative pronoun], places, sides, highway, banks, purple, crops, that [relative pronoun], rows, lace-work, ground, trees, sunlight, meanest, them.

Of these seventeen nouns/pronouns, eight of them (47%) function as the objects of a preposition:

> places, sides, highway, purple, lace-work, ground, sunlight, them.

---

[9]Ibid., 13.

[10]Robert Fitzgerald, intro., *Everything That Rises Must Converge* by Flannery O'Connor (New York: Farrar, Straus, and Giroux, 1965) xi.

Selecting the remaining nouns/pronouns left to carry the force of O'Connor's message yields the following list:

> Mountain, granite, that [relative pronoun], banks, crops, that [relative pronoun], rows, trees, meanest.

Through syntactic diminishment the force of the image becomes absorbed into the prepositional phrases and adjectival modifiers. The intensity of these images, which might lead O'Connor's readers to perceive Christ as ever present in their world, thus significantly declines in vitality.

The compelling power of religious overtones possible in O'Connor's landscape images also dwindles because of an unexpected doctrinal emphasis often suggested through her choice of adjectives, adverbs, and verbs. In "The Partridge Festival" Calhoun wakes to find that "a slow rain was descending indifferently," and that "The rain has beat the azaleas down" (*CS* 437; 438). The fact that the rain, which could serve as the life-giving nourishment to both the land and its people, descends "indifferently" obscures in lethargy any connection to its absolving power to sanctify. And the use of the verb "beat" as nature's treatment of one of her own emphasizes the terrible avenging power unleashed upon the earth, a power that batters and destroys. Once again, O'Connor's God, if he can be seen at all in this nature imagery, is either presented as unconcerned about his creatures or raging and angry as was the God who sent the flood waters to descend upon Noah. Readers anticipating a modern-day Christian interpretation within O'Connor's world would certainly have difficulty contemplating her God as the One with whom they are familiar. In fact, her images extolling a God who is slow and indifferent to his creations might even cause readers to shun any connection to this God they believed left with the Old Testament.

In "Greenleaf," when Mrs. May looks out at her cows in the pastures, she finds them fenced in by "a black wall of trees with a sharp sawtooth edge that held off the indifferent sky" (*CS* 321). The trees, which in religious imagery often signify the presence of Christ's suffering in this world, in O'Connor's world are themselves instruments of danger. And the modality of this sentence, which is once again determined by O'Connor's choice of the adjective "indifferent," fails to clarify the image of "sky" as potentially god-like because of the conflicting modern perspective of a caring God actively aware of the fate of his flock. The reader perceives the heaven encased within this sky as uncaring through word choices that indicate a deliberate detachment. Additionally, the "sharp sawtooth edge" of the trees overrides any traditional Christian imagery we might expect to find in "trees" were they to behave as images of Christ's cross.

In "Greenleaf," O'Connor's bull may be viewed as a Christ-figure because of the surrounding imagery of the crown of thorns around his head and the continuation of his mission for three days. Yet O'Connor insinuates ambiguity in this imagery. The bull is continually associated with images of lowering and darkness, both images allied with Satan. Does she mean for us to envision the bull as Christ who with lowered head prayed in the Garden of Gethsemane and who with lowered head at the moment of his ultimate sacrifice on the cross died for the sins of all humans? Or are we to envision the bull as representing Lucifer, Prince of Darkness, emboweled in the depths of hell? In "Greenleaf" the images of darkness surrounding the bull dominate, confusing the interpretation of the image by presenting a picture of God as a power more menacing than redemptive. When the story opens, the bull is dramatically equated with darkness and evil:

> Clouds . . . blackened him and in the dark he began to tear at the hedge.
>
> He took a step backward and lowered his head . . .
>
> The bull lowered his head and shook it and the wreath slipped down to the base of his horns where it looked like a menacing prickly crown. (*CS* 311; 311; 312)

As Mrs. May and Mr. Greenleaf prepare to destroy this "heavy form," this "iron shadow [that] moved away in the darkness," O'Connor describes him as being "dark among the spotted cows" (*CS* 329; 331). And when the bull is ready to claim his victim, O'Connor introduces him thus:

> In a few minutes something emerged from the tree line, a black heavy shadow that tossed its head several times and then bounded forward. After a second she saw it was the bull. (*CS* 333)

One would expect the bull, if its role is to be a Christ-figure, to achieve a position of some prominence in this descriptive passage. Yet, O'Connor waits until the second sentence to introduce the noun "the bull." The potency of this Christ imagery is displaced by her decision to use the words "something" and "a black heavy shadow" as the reader's first introduction to the bull as he attempts to complete his mission to thrust Mrs. May full of grace. Even when O'Connor does finally use the noun "bull" to refer to Mrs. May's fictional redeemer, she syntactically blurs its focus by hiding the noun as a predicate nominative within a subordinate clause whose subject is "it." Frederick Asals writes that "Without ever ceasing to be a plausible farm animal, the bull takes on the burden of another dimension."[11] And this is perhaps what O'Connor intended. But the layers of language one must uncover in search of her message entangle the reader in a misleading syntax and a confusing imagistic association between divine and satanic forces.

When Christ is mentioned in her fiction, the Christ that O'Connor writes of is often an eccentric figure who is continually referenced unexpectedly. In *Wise Blood* when Haze remembers his grandfather lying in his coffin, he remembers that he

> had been a circuit preacher, a waspish old man who had ridden over three counties with Jesus hidden in his head like a stinger. (*Collected* 9-10)

As is evident in O'Connor's letter to John Hawkes in 1962, critics did not come easily to her intended meanings. In defense of her novelistic intentions, O'Connor reacted to Hawkes's judgment of her atypical images:

> Isn't it arbitrary to call these images such as . . . the grandfather who went around with Jesus hidden in his head like a stinger—perverse? They are right, accurate, so why perverse? . . . Nobody with a religious consciousness is going to call these images perverse and mean that they are really perverse. What I mean to say is that when you call them perverse, you are departing from that word's traditional meaning. (*Collected* 1160)

[11]Frederick Asals, *Flannery O'Connor: The Imagination of Extremity* (Athens: University of Georgia Press, 1982) 74.

Yet they often are cruel, violent, and unorthodox, and in their startling originality they may lead the reader into assuming that their meanings are equally unorthodox.

As Haze continues to reflect on the strict religious upbringing of his childhood, he remembers that his grandfather used to preach from the top of his Ford automobile to those who would listen about a "soul-hungry" Jesus. This Jesus, this "wild ragged figure,"

> would chase him over the waters of sin! . . . Jesus would never let him forget he was redeemed. What did the sinner think there was to be gained? Jesus would have him in the end. (*Collected* 11)

The Jesus O'Connor creates in her fiction is a necessary hunter of souls for those gone astray, a Jesus reminiscent of Thompson's "Hound of Heaven" or Hopkins's "devouring" Christ. O'Connor was so concerned that her duty as an author was to jar her audience into an awareness of their iniquities that her God could ill afford to wait patiently for his flock to mend their ways. O'Connor's Christ must be as perverse a figure as Hawkes envisioned and the Augustinian influence demanded. Her Jesus must seek and destroy, for to do otherwise would result in a further loss of souls. The implications of the more modern, gentle Christ who lovingly watches over his lambs, the theological Christ with whom O'Connor's audience would be acquainted, in O'Connor's opinion would necessarily result in a continuation of the status quo. In O'Connor's scheme, it is logical that Hazel Motes, faced with this feckless Jesus, became a preacher for his "Church Without Christ."

Haze preaches that

> The Church Without Christ don't have a Jesus but it needs one! It needs a new jesus! It needs one that's all man, without blood to waste, and it needs one that don't look like any other man so you'll look at him. Give me such a jesus, you people. Give me such a new jesus and you'll see how far the Church Without Christ can go! (*Collected* 80)

Enoch, listening to Haze preach, is much like O'Connor's reader. He misunderstands Haze's real intentions and recasts this new Jesus as the bloodless mummy that once was all man, that now looks like no other.

O'Connor has Haze preach that "Nothing matters but that Jesus was a liar" (*Collected* 59). And Haze even makes the statement that "Blasphemy is the way to the truth" when combating Onnie Jay Holy's attempt to turn his "Church Without Christ" into a money-grubbing scam (*Collected* 86). Onnie Jay's Jesus is, in fact, a liar; his "truth" is a profound blasphemy. Thus, for Haze to blaspheme the blasphemy of the modern Church is to seek for truth. Yet, O'Connor's unsettling rhetorical conjectures and profane images, which conjure up a Jesus unfamiliar to modern Christian readers, reinforce confusion in readers trying to reconcile O'Connor's Augustinian imagery with emerging Vatican II Catholic dogma.

Similar images of a traditionally blasphemous nature exist in O'Connor's second novel. In *The Violent Bear It Away* when Tarwater realizes his vocation is to baptize Bishop he knows that

> he was called to be a prophet and that the ways of his prophecy would not be remarkable. His black pupils, glassy and still, reflected depth on depth his own stricken image of himself, trudging into the distance in the bleeding stinking mad shadow of Jesus, until at last he received his reward, a broken fish, a multiplied loaf. (*Collected* 389)

Tarwater, like Haze before him, envisions Jesus as a bleeding, stinking madman who rewards his followers with one broken fish, one multiplied loaf. Here the imagery appropriates traditional Christian imagery of a bleeding Christ who fed the multitudes with a few fish and loaves of bread. Yet O'Connor turns this image into a repulsive physical presence that mocks the reader with a reward that linguistically cannot satisfy—"a broken fish, a multiplied loaf," an image that becomes stripped of its miraculous nature to feed the body and heal the spirit.

O'Connor's theology compels that God stalk and exterminate the Raybers, the Mrs. Mays, the Mrs. Turpins we have all become. For those schooled in a more humanistic view of Christianity, however, her vision becomes impenetrable. O'Connor's macabre images of the Christian Savior, sustained by juxtaposition with other incongruous images, impede customary Christian or Catholic perceptions. The reader, faced with O'Connor's profane imagination of a Christian (Haze, The Misfit, the Tarwaters) and her shocking parody of subversion embodied in her image of Christ himself, may "rewrite" O'Connor's story as a satire on religion and an irreverent mockery of those fundamentalist imaginations of God.

O'Connor's story of the grandmother and The Misfit introduces images that connect characters with lifeless materials and objects and often deny them their spirituality. In "A Good Man Is Hard to Find" the grandmother's face is described as leathery, and the family passes by a graveyard with "five or six graves fenced in the middle of it" (*CS* 119). Perhaps O'Connor means to indicate the spiritual condition of her characters. The grandmother is spiritually like a dead animal, only realized religiously, at this point in her existence, as an empty outer covering. She is, perhaps, no better than Enoch's mummy with a head full of trash. This inanimate imagery appears to reinforce O'Connor's view that these characters have not yet received their moments of grace. Here the grandmother is not in possession of the necessary grace to attain salvation (the other family members are never fully developed in this regard). But O'Connor's obvious foreshadowing of the graves that will soon be needed for the grandmother's family sets up ambiguity as to the grandmother's redemptive fate. The graveyard the family passes had "five or six graves" in it. Will the sixth grave be needed for the grandmother, the sixth member of the family, or will she be resurrected from her life of pious indifference to the true meaning of Christianity and, therefore, need no earthly grave? To the reader O'Connor's images often appear to be at cross purposes.

While en route to their portentous destiny, the grandmother's family stops at "a part stucco and part wood filling station" for sandwiches, and the family sits down at a "board table" (*CS* 120; 121). As they drive off to continue their trip, the grandmother tells of a house she wants them to visit (the pursuit of which will unknowingly cause their doom), describing it as having "six white columns . . . and two little wooden trellis arbors on either side in front" (*CS* 123). She tells about the family silver hidden in the house which excites John Wesley who wants to "poke all the woodwork and find it!" (*CS* 123). Bailey, to stop his children's bickering, turns "onto the dirt road and the car raced roughly along in a swirl of pink dust" to where their accident occurs, and where the family will collide with The Misfit and his murderous cohorts (*CS* 124). The grandmother's vision of the house she yearns to visit can be viewed as her unconscious desire to realize entrance into God's mansion in the sky for herself and her family. O'Connor once again punctuates her descriptions with landscape images omnipresent in her Georgia surroundings. But in religious terms, she may have intended for the many images of wood and dirt and pink dust to take on additional meanings as indications of God's awareness of the frailty of his creatures and of his Son's mission to suffer and die for all humankind. In this story, once again O'Connor reduces the intensity of her images by burying them in prepositional phrases or hiding them as descriptive adjectives.

John Hawkes writes that O'Connor's "extreme absurdity of juxtaposing the human and the inanimate" leads to "the creation of flat personality."[12] Images of metals, wood and paper products, concrete, stucco, clay, dirt, stone, and granite, which are so prevalent throughout O'Connor's fiction, create conditions that intrinsically connect lifeless substances with creatures usually presumed to have the potential for spiritual life. While it is unlikely O'Connor intended this imagery to detract from her message, damnation and inanimate imagery ostensibly meld in "A Good Man Is Hard to Find" and in most of her fiction. O'Connor's infusion into her text of descriptive images with inanimate references undermines any sentiments of expected Christian humanism. O'Connor's fictional images, therefore, more readily convey an attitude toward salvation that can be interpreted as nullifying redemptive opportunities.

Rufus Johnson, in "The Lame Shall Enter First," is one of O'Connor's characters who is continually connected with inanimate materials. O'Connor's first personal description of Johnson describes his eyes as "steel-colored" (*CS* 449). As his character becomes realized in the story, and he first enters Sheppard's home, Johnson terrorizes Norton by rifling through his dead mother's closet where he finds and puts on her "faded corset with four dangling metal supporters" (*CS* 456). And when Sheppard puts his hand on Johnson's forehead trying to assure him that he is convinced of his innocence concerning a second break-in report, Johnson's forehead is described as "cold and dry like rusty iron" (*CS* 469).

Sheppard later takes Johnson to the brace shop, "a small concrete warehouse," and there Johnson sits on a "plastic-cushioned" chair. His shoe is described as patched "with a piece of canvas" and "the two sides were laced with twine" (*CS* 470). When Johnson lies to Sheppard about his complicity in the break-in, he relates in his own defense: "There wasn't any tracks. That whole place is concreted in the back and my feet were dry" (*CS* 473). He then infuriates Sheppard by insisting on his belief in the Bible, and to demonstrate this he tears a page and chews and swallows the paper. After he is caught by the police, Johnson states his reason for his crime: "To show up that big tin Jesus!" (*CS* 480). O'Connor has Johnson himself state his spiritual condition: "When I get ready to be saved, Jesus'll save me," a statement reminiscent of the

[12] Hawkes, "Flannery O'Connor's Devil," 14-15.

Protestant's "personal salvation" and of the Protestant tenet that faith alone (without good works) is all that is necessary for salvation (*CS* 480).

Miles Orvell considers Johnson one of O'Connor's "prophet freaks who (the will being free) does *not* undergo a conversion experience" and who is "yet unpossessed of grace."[13] O'Connor has not made Johnson's will free, but it is not clear that he remains unredeemed since he brings Norton to reverence for the heavens and exposes to Sheppard the cold evil of what he thought were "good works." Johnson's philosophy of "personal salvation," his connection with constrictive brace and corset imagery, and the inanimate word-pictures that join Johnson's soul irrevocably to non-living materials combine to shroud O'Connor's message in mystery. The confusion revolves around the fact that despite the imagery that could be interpreted as damning, it is Johnson and not Sheppard who actually "knows" Christ. Johnson is connected with the imagery associated with lifelessness, yet it is Sheppard who is spiritually dead and who must be taught the supreme lesson.

In discussing "Good Country People" O'Connor details the symbolism that she employed in her development of Hulga:

> there is a wooden part of her soul that corresponds to her wooden leg. Now of course this is never stated. The fiction writer states as little as possible. The reader makes this connection from things he is shown. (*MM* 99)

In addition to this interpretation of the symbolic meaning of Hulga's artificial leg, made of wooden materials, "wood" in O'Connor's fiction seems indicative of the presence of Christ in his redemptive role. She explicitly makes this connection of woods and trees to Christ in another story in a December 1956 letter to "A": "The name of the story is a view of the woods and the woods alone are pure enough to be a Christ symbol if anything is" (*HB* 190). But "wood" also assumes significance as imagery. O'Connor's explanation of Hulga's "wooden part of her soul" legitimizes the use of "wood" and other inanimate imagery that will be associated with her and with the Bible salesman, and that will present pictures of their immortal souls.

After the Bible salesman removes Hulga's leg, which literally cripples her, his eyes are described as being like "two steel spikes" (*CS* 289).

---

[13]Orvell, *Invisible Parade*, 44.

Only Hulga, to whom O'Connor allows the possibility of achieving redemption, is wrenched from a connection with inanimate materials. Does O'Connor intend the theft of her wooden leg to shake Hulga out of her nihilistic complacency, freeing her from its wooden burden which will at last allow the pursuit of salvation by presumably leaving her open to an influx of grace? Or is the reader to see the removal of the redemptive cross from her spiritual future? Because O'Connor's images do not remain static, the reader may instead see Hulga, the hulking, ugly nihilist, as annihilated by her own beliefs and forever shut out of God's kingdom. The fact is that wooden imagery, which sometimes signifies the saving cross of Christ, and sometimes the "wooden soul" of her characters, continually sets up turmoil in the minds of O'Connor's readers trying to achieve a consistency of image and meaning.

The difficulty of understanding O'Connor's images becomes most problematical in her imagery of death and destruction since the question of what is being destroyed or born in its place is so thematically important. The imagery surrounding The Misfit and his companions illustrates the confusion. In "A Good Man Is Hard to Find" when the three killers approach the family in "a big black battered hearse-like automobile," O'Connor describes Bobby Lee, one of the escaped convicts, as wearing "a red sweat shirt with a silver stallion embossed on the front of it," and she describes The Misfit as "holding a black hat and a gun" (*CS* 126). These images apparently derive from the Apocalypse (silver, death, horses, black) but does O'Connor mean them to announce the triumph of evil as in the Four Horsemen of the Apocalypse, or the revelation of Christ's grace at the moment of judgment?

How to read The Misfit's connection with images of earth and death remains enigmatic. For the seven remaining pages of the story O'Connor emphasizes The Misfit's connections to earth with imagery that aligns him intimately with burials and death both physically and spiritually. As an escaped convict, he buried his clothes; as an undertaker, he buried people; and as a prisoner in the penitentiary, he was buried alive. Do these images make him an embodiment of death, or one resurrected from it? In the first two burial images, The Misfit participated in the performance of the burial act. In the penitentiary image, however, the passive construction indicates that The Misfit did not perform the action (was not penitential), but was, in fact, buried by someone or something. The Misfit seems not in control of his destiny; on the other hand, he is the active killer of the victimized family. Unless the reader is aware that O'Connor intends The Misfit ultimately to join the Resurrection, the emphasis on death and burial images creates a linguistic diversion masking the conception of a resurrection that belongs to those "born again" in the spirit of Christ.

O'Connor believed that violence, though sometimes distasteful, was an instrument aiding salvation. She wrote in *Mystery and Manners*: "in my own stories I have found that violence is strangely capable of returning my characters to reality and preparing them to accept their moment of grace" (*MM* 112). Feeley cites this very quotation in her support of O'Connor's explanation: "The story leaves open the possibility that the grandmother's mysterious action of love will open the Misfit's mind to the reality of mystery."[14] Feeley continues to use O'Connor's explications as her touchstone. She writes that

> the Misfit is a "good man" in many respects. The author draws him with compassion and puts him far ahead of Bailey and Red Sammy in gentleness and politeness.[15]

The reader can only wonder if the grandmother and her family would agree with this assessment.

Feeley's reading is typical of that from critics who accept O'Connor's explanations as to what her stories mean. However, a reader not privy to such justification may find few reasons to vindicate The Misfit for the grandmother's murder. To most readers the superficial context surrounding the words "politeness" and "gentleness" do not equate to the virtue of "goodness" which, in The Misfit, has become unrecognizable. Only after the grandmother's touch and her subsequent murder does O'Connor ascribe to this killer what may be reported minimally as regret. Feeley, however, sees The Misfit's role in O'Connor's terms. She writes that

> The Misfit's comment, "She would of been a good woman . . . if it had been somebody there to shoot her every minute of her life," indicates that he understands the impact of violence which has ended her alienation by returning her to reality and transformed her from a "lady" to a "good woman."[16]

---

[14]Feeley, *Voice of the Peacock*, 75.
[15]Ibid., 74.
[16]Ibid., 73.

While O'Connor does, in fact, consider The Misfit a modern-day Lazarus who will be resurrected through the grandmother's touch, the reader is constantly confronted with images that confound this reading. The Misfit does tell the grandmother that "Jesus was the only One that ever raised the dead," which obviously indicates his awareness that only Jesus can offer salvation to his creatures (*CS* 132). However, The Misfit's statement is followed by several conditional situations. The Misfit says:

> If He did what He said, then it's nothing for you to do but throw away everything and follow Him, and if He didn't then it's nothing for you to do but enjoy the few minutes you got left the best way you can—by killing somebody or burning down his house or doing some other meanness to him. (*CS* 132)

The story ends with three more sentences spoken by The Misfit:

> "She would of been a good woman," The Misfit said, "if it had been somebody there to shoot her every minute of her life."
> "Some fun!" Bobby Lee said.
> "Shut up, Bobby Lee," The Misfit said. "It's no real pleasure in life." (*CS* 133)

From the first "if" statement on page 132 (quoted above) until the end of the story, The Misfit voices his thoughts in eight sentences. Within these sentences he uses the word "if" five times. Additionally, the grandmother responds to these conditionals with the statement that "Maybe He didn't raise the dead," another provisional proposition (*CS* 132). Even the surrounding narrative emphasizes the tentativeness of this world, for O'Connor writes that The Misfit's face was "twisted . . . as if he were going to cry" (*CS* 132). But was he? And after the grandmother reaches out to touch him, O'Connor writes that he "sprang back as if a snake had bitten him" (*CS* 132). But had it? In these statements O'Connor leaves a syntactical uncertainty about the spiritual disposition of characters who despite their questioning of an unjust world, must commit injustices such as murder to reveal a God of Love.

Feeley insists O'Connor's fictional explanations assure that The Misfit, given the proper conditions, will throw down everything and follow Him. However, once again the language and imagery slip away from O'Connor's conscious constraints. The transformation the reader is asked to consider as a definition of a "good man" is not that the grandmother has been changed from a shallow self-centered "lady" to a caring spiritual being, but rather that The Misfit has been transformed from a heartless killer to a member of the Resurrection. Within O'Connor's framework, and in her assessment, The Misfit is to come from the dead as one of those resurrected through Christ; he will follow Him. One wonders, however, if Lazarus had been a sociopath or a perverted child killer, would the biblical story have worked as a parable? As Orvell writes:

> With O'Connor, as with other writers of firm belief (Dante, for example), the unassailable dramatic image is closer to the vision than any doctrinal equivalent. . . . In O'Connor's best fiction too, it is "the image that is the reality."[17]

Readers must question the kind of deity who manifests his grace through depraved crimes and sees the "good man" in a killer of children. While O'Connor believed that experiencing grace and salvation through violent means was a way to rescue irreligious beings antagonistic towards salvation from certain damnation, her images fail to provide insights that can transform violent behavior into conduct overtly recognized as divine. Thus O'Connor's fictional reality, wherein the perpetrators of violence are afforded the same salvific consideration afforded the victims, becomes troublesome. O'Connor's images do more to displace the power embodied literally and figuratively in Christ's resurrection than to embrace it.

[17]Orvell, *Invisible Parade*, 27.

4. Catholic Themes in the Works of O'Connor

O'Connor was not, nor did she intend to be, perceived as typical. In fact during the early stages of her first novel, *Wise Blood*, O'Connor changed publishing firms because, in her opinion, her first publisher wanted her to alter her novel into something quite ordinary, a situation she felt compelled to resist. She relayed her consternation regarding the publisher's reception of her novel to John Selby of Rinehart:

> I can only hope that in the finished novel the direction will be clearer, but I can tell you that I would not like at all to work with you as do other writers on your list. I feel that whatever virtues the novel may have are very much connected with the limitations you mention. I am not writing a conventional novel, and I think that the quality of the novel I write will derive precisely from the peculiarity or aloneness, if you will, of the experience I write from. . . .
>
> In short, I am amenable to criticism but only within the sphere of what I am trying to do; I will not be persuaded to do otherwise. The finished book, though I hope less angular, will be just as odd if not odder than the nine chapters you have now. (*HB* 10)

In addition to "making up a good case for distortion as . . . the only way to make people see," O'Connor had a certain aversion to being perceived as simply a Catholic writer and, therefore, a writer expected to have a plainly orthodox agenda (*HB* 79). Writing to Andrew Lytle in 1955, she emphasized her desire to escape the restrictive perceptions an audience would assign to writers they viewed as representing either the provincialism determined by locale or by belief:

> To my way of thinking, the only thing that keeps me from being a regional writer is being a Catholic and the only thing that keeps me from being a Catholic writer (in the narrow sense) is being a Southerner . . . (*HB* 104)

O'Connor wished to be considered an artist with a universal message. On occasion, O'Connor, therefore, would even deny that she was a Catholic writer. She writes of this in 1959 to John Hawkes:

> People are always asking me if I am a Catholic writer and I am afraid that I sometimes say no and sometimes say yes, depending entirely on who the visitor is. Actually, the question seems so remote from what I am doing when I am doing it, that it doesn’t bother me at all. (*Collected* 1109-1110)

O’Connor considered that pigeon-holing artists as Southern, or Catholic, limited both their reception and their perceived greatness. But more importantly, she believed people no longer intimately acquainted with religion in their daily lives would have difficulty relating to fictional works that touted religious ideas and ideals either as the norm or as a necessity. O’Connor felt that the greatest religious impact she could achieve in a world desperately devoid of religion could only be accomplished by presenting religion as anti-religion, or at the very least by shrouding her mores and morals in a microcosm which when carefully scrutinized would perhaps reveal the Divine Mystery through a recognition of opposites. She emphasized this in *Mystery and Manners* when she wrote that a great novel must incorporate a “realism which does not hesitate to distort appearances in order to show a hidden truth” (*MM* 179).

O’Connor felt very strongly that the fiction writer must write so that “when he finishes there always has to be left over that sense of Mystery which cannot be accounted for by any human formula” (*MM* 153). O’Connor’s conscious, concerted effort to shift the emphasis away from conventional, doctrinal Catholicism caused her to transmit her fictional message in a linguistically covert fashion. This attempt at diverting attention away from any obvious connection with traditional Catholic doctrine, coupled with her unorthodox treatment of the sacraments and other religious ideas and symbols, may also lead readers away from the Christianity and Catholicism she wished to bring them to value. Still, O’Connor meant her fiction to sustain the Catholic view, for as she stated in *Habit of Being*: “My background and my inclinations are both Catholic and I think this is very apparent in the book [*Wise Blood*]” (*HB* 68).

Not all readers or critics see *Wise Blood* her way, however, as John Desmond’s comments illustrate: “Even though at the end Haze becomes one of O’Connor’s crypto-Catholics, there are no sacraments in his world, no 'outward sign' that can be the media of grace."[1] O'Connor's authorial inclinations are more internally contradictory than her statements sometimes acknowledge, a condition that may account in part for the failure of her stories to carry the burden of her doctrine. The previous chapters have considered several reasons why disagreement abounds among O'Connor's critics as to the integrity of her fiction to fictional expressions accepted as Catholic. This chapter will delve into her treatment of Catholic values as O'Connor presents them in her fictional representations.

O'Connor's fictional treatment of such sacraments as marriage, for example, so alters the spiritual context that readers may arrive at the conclusion that O'Connor does not share the traditional Catholic view of this aspect of doctrine. Christ's first miracle was performed at a wedding ceremony in Cana of Galilee because of his mother's compassion for the bridal couple and her impassioned entreaty, "They have no wine." Catholics have traditionally interpreted the performance of this miracle at a wedding as evidence of Christ's elevation of the institution of marriage to sacramental status. The traditional social view of marriage as a sacrament of love, and the religious view that it is one of the seven sacraments of the Catholic Church, are not readily perceived in O'Connor's fiction, however. In fact, most of her stories involve main characters who are widows or widowers. Only four of O'Connor's stories mention a marriage relationship: "The Displaced Person" and "A Stroke of Good Fortune," which appear in *A Good Man Is Hard to Find*, published in 1955; and "Revelation" and "Parker's Back," which appear in *Everything That Rises Must Converge*, published posthumously in 1965. These stories vary widely as to the emphasis placed on the actual marriage, and only one ("Parker's Back") embodies what O'Connor considers a blessed marriage. In most of these stories, marriage is either a mockery or a unification of the damned. Even in "Parker's Back" where marriage redeems, the portrait of the "loving" couple may seem more masochistic than Christian.

During a Catholic Mass for the Bride and Bridegroom, as it would have been performed during O'Connor's lifetime, the priest's proclamation that "a man shall leave his father and mother, and cleave to his wife" conveys not only the sanction of physical closeness now permitted by the laws of the Church with the receipt of this sacrament, but also conveys

[1] John F. Desmond, *Risen Sons: Flannery O'Connor's Vision of History* (Athens: University of Georgia Press, 1987) 61.

the urging of spiritual, and emotional closeness as well.[2] The epistle read during this ceremony comes from "The Epistle of St Paul the Apostle to the Ephesians" which begins:

> Brethren: Let wives be subject to their husbands as to the Lord: because a husband is head of the wife, just as Christ is head of the Church, being Himself Savior of the body. But just as the Church is subject to Christ, so also let wives be to their husbands in all things.[3]

O'Connor's wives seem not to have taken note of this charge of the pre-Vatican II Catholic Church.

In "The Displaced Person" Mrs. McIntyre, a widow, remembers marrying her husband, the Judge, because "she had liked him" (*CS* 218). Yet O'Connor describes her deceased first husband as "a dirty snuff-dipping Court House figure" who

> left her a mortgaged house and fifty acres that he had managed to cut the timber off before he died. It was as if, as the final triumph of a successful life, he had been able to take everything with him. (*CS* 218)

The suggestion of the Judge's skulduggery, even in death, at the expense of his wife's well-being, leaves the reader with a damning portrait of marriage. Mrs. McIntyre's succeeding attempts at matrimony, producing second and third husbands who ended up either "in the state asylum" or intoxicated "in some hotel room in Florida," do little to generate a reversal of the already established negative attitude toward marriage as an institution (*CS* 218). Her failure to achieve a Christian marriage may at one level be an indication of the state of Mrs. McIntyre's soul, but the picture of marriage within the story also sets up an attitude toward marriage that extends beyond the failures of Mrs. McIntyre's character.

In this same story, O'Connor outlines the relationship of another couple, Mr. and Mrs. Shortley, in more detail. Mrs. Shortley is described in the opening paragraph as "the giant wife of the countryside" who

---

[2]Hugo H. Hoever, editor, *Saint Joseph Daily Missal* (New York: Catholic Book Publishing Co., 1957) 598.

[3]Ibid., 597.

> rose, . . . surveying everything. She ignored the white afternoon sun which was creeping behind a ragged wall of cloud as if it pretended to be an intruder and cast her gaze down the red clay road that turned off from the highway. (*CS* 194)

Mrs. Shortley's power is without compare in Mr. Shortley's eyes for he "had never in his life doubted her omniscience" (*CS* 212). In fact, throughout the story, Mrs. Shortley is intimately connected with the verb "knew":

> Mrs. Shortley knew they [the Negroes] were there.
>
> which Mrs. Shortley knew, was what priests did . . .
>
> she knew that if Mrs. McIntyre had considered her trash, they couldn't have talked about trashy people together.
>
> "I know what Sledgewig told Annie Maude," she said . . .
>
> "I known he was taking turkeys."
>
> She knew something the Displaced Person was doing that would floor Mrs. McIntyre.
>
> Mrs. Shortley nodded to indicate she had known this for some time. (*CS* 194; 195; 202-203; 204; 207; 208; 208)

Even the young black farm worker, Sulk, associates Mrs. Shortley with the verb "know" when he says, "Big Belly act like she know everything" (*CS* 206). And in fact, she feels she does. For she knows in her heart that

> she had a special part in [God's] plan because she was strong. She saw that the Lord God Almighty had created the strong people to do what had to be done and she felt that she would be ready when she was called. (*CS* 209)

These characteristics of strength and knowing are lacking in Mr. Shortley. In many ways, Mrs. Shortley's marriage is very similar to the marriage of Claud and Ruby Turpin (discussed below). Mr. Shortley does tricks with a cigarette and Mrs. Shortley could "hug him to death" because of his comic ability. Yet Mr. Shortley, like Claud, appears to be the weaker partner physically: he “had been in bed two days with an attack” because of “over-exhaustion” (*CS* 204). Once Mrs. Shortley even had to assume his duties and “drive in the cows for Mr. Shortley who had a pain in his knee” (*CS* 210). While there does seem to be affection between the couple, and Mr. Shortley does experience sorrow at his wife’s death, he is never afforded any authority in their marriage. Mrs. Shortly never assumes a posture of subservience as the epistle of St. Paul solicits and traditional Catholics would have expected in the 1950s and 1960s.

As they go to bed, Mrs. Shortley tries to warn her husband that Mr. Guizac might reveal the existence of his whisky still to Mrs. McIntyre. But O’Connor sets up a lack of interaction between the couple: “Mr. Shortley folded his hands on his bony chest and pretended he was a corpse” (*CS* 206). When Mr. Shortley will not respond, Mrs. Shortley gives him “a sharp kick in the side with her knee” and demands that he answer her; his response is only, “‘Don’t worry me now. . . . I’m a dead man’” (*CS* 206). O’Connor continues with this analogy by having Mr. Shortley reemphasize that “‘If everybody was as dead as I am, nobody would have no trouble’” (*CS* 206).

Mrs. Shortley totally controls her husband. When she overhears Mrs. McIntyre say that he will be given one month’s notice, she takes it upon herself to make the decision that the family will leave before her husband can be fired. Mr. Shortley, without input into the decision to leave or remain, obeys his wife’s directives, helps pack their belongings, gets into the car and begins driving away before he asks her “‘Where we goin?’” (*CS* 213).

Not until after Mrs. Shortley’s death, does Mr. Shortley finally act like one alive. Once he is away from her overpowering domination, which is only achieved through *her* becoming a corpse, is he finally able to have a capacity for knowledge and action. He now interacts with Mrs. McIntyre and becomes irritated by her repeated inability to fire Mr. Guizac despite her insistence that she will do so. Mr. Shortley tells himself that:

> he should have known all along that no woman was going to do what she said she was when she said she was. He didn’t know how long he could afford to put up with her shilly-shallying. (*CS* 228)

Since the death of his wife, Mr. Shortley assumes control of his situation:

> Mr. Shortley began to come to [Mrs. McIntyre's] back door every evening to put certain facts before her. . . . [and] he could watch her face and tell he was making an impression. (*CS* 228)

Freed from the shackles of his marriage, which is emphasized by the use of the reflexive pronoun, O'Connor writes that, "Mr. Shortley himself did things as he pleased" (*CS* 230).

Even a "happy" marriage may for O'Connor be the setting for sins against God. "A Stroke of Good Fortune" is one of O'Connor's most explicit endorsements of Catholic doctrine, but the way in which the story is told leaves the wife, who has been forced to the terms of the sacramental nature of marriage, in a dazed state of horror and despair.

Ruby Hill, in "A Stroke of Good Fortune," is happy with her husband, Bill Hill, because she feels he has removed her from her meager beginnings. She is happy because her marriage, in her estimation, has elevated her status, allowing her to become "better" than her relations. Yet for Ruby, marriage does not encompass the possibility of conception, a very un-Catholic attitude since a Catholic marriage is not considered consummated until the sexual act has been performed, and this act must never dictate to God by thwarting the prospect of procreation.

Despite intimations that they seem to enjoy a happy relationship, Bill Hill and Ruby do not agree on the Catholic meaning of marriage. Catholics in O'Connor's day would be familiar with the implicit doctrine to be formally endorsed in the papal encyclical *Humanae Vitae* issued in 1968 by Pope Paul VI that "reiterated the Church's traditional ban on the use of artificial contraceptives," and held that "every conjugal act must be open to the transmission of life."[4] Portrayals of a marriage that rejected life would run counter to traditional Catholic doctrine. Yet Ruby and Bill Hill have been practicing birth control. Bill Hill, the partner responsible for choosing their birth-control method, has "slipped up" and caused Ruby to get pregnant. Ruby, vehement in her dislike of children, had approved the use of birth control, an act not only counter to Catholic teaching, but an act categorically labeled in Catholic terms as a mortal sin. When she first becomes aware that she may be pregnant, Ruby, in panic, wildly disclaims:

---

[4]Deedy, *The Catholic Fact Book,* 179.

> "Not me!" Ruby shouted. "Oh, no not me! Bill Hill takes care of that. Bill Hill takes care of that! Bill Hill's been taking care of that for five years! That ain't going to happen to me!" (*Collected* 193)

The story continues to rail against motherhood by making constant and inconsistent references to its trials and tribulations. Ruby remembers the horrors her own mother endured through the experience of having children:

> she had always looked sour, she had always looked like she wasn't satisfied with anything. . . . All those children were what did her mother in—eight of them: two born dead, one died the first year, one crushed under a mowing machine. Her mother had got deader with every one of them. And all of it for what? (*Collected* 186)

The images of an unhappy family life skew Ruby's view of marriage. But while this makes her a bad Catholic, it also makes her resistance to childbirth a more humanly understandable response. When Ruby finally comes to the realization that she is pregnant, she denies her state:

> No. No. It couldn't be any baby. She was not going to have something waiting in her to make her deader, she was not. (*Collected* 195)

Ruby cancels any recognition of the life within her by referring to her baby as "something," not "someone." From the point at which she becomes aware that she is probably pregnant, every sentence that Ruby thinks or speaks, except for four, contains negative words. She either uses a verb in the negative form, the expletive "no," or words with negative connotation such as "just" in the sense of "only." This narrative choice, in itself, is not unusual because Ruby is in a state of shock at her unwanted condition, and denial is understandable. But more important than Ruby's words are the negative images that O'Connor presents as impressionistic accompaniments.

The story begins and ends with Ruby on the stairs. At the opening, Ruby is climbing the stairs to reach her apartment. Thomas Fawcett states that in the language of religion: "The imagery of a ladder or stairway often appears, for it is an obvious way of suggesting a means of connection between the worlds of gods and men."[5] However, O'Connor uses the stairway "up" only to reinforce its opposite. By the end of the story, Ruby looks "down into the stairwell," and she gives a "long hollow wail" in a "stair cavern [that] was dark green and mole-colored" (*Collected* 195). She refuses the ladder to heaven.

The reader's final impression of the story is embodied in the appearance of Hartley Gilfeet. Hartley is the epitome of the unruly, disrespectful, brat of a boy. His very existence portends what Ruby's unborn child could become, a prospect to strike fear in the heart of any expectant mother. When Hartley knocks Ruby onto the stairs, O'Connor confers a further inhuman and certainly unlovable image of him as having "a charging chipmunk face" while Ruby, "clutching the banister," out of breath, "gazed down into the dark hole, down to the very bottom where she had started up so long ago" (*Collected* 196). As she looks downward, in "the dark hole," Ruby, who carries the beginnings of life within her, hears her own voice echo down the stairwell, "'Good Fortune, Baby,'" as a leer rather than the cheer of a woman ecstatic over the impending birth of her child. O'Connor's final image of Ruby is as she experiences the quickening of life:

> Then she recognized the feeling again, a little roll. It was as if it were not in her stomach. It was as if it were out nowhere in nothing, out nowhere, resting and waiting, with plenty of time. (*Collected* 196)

O'Connor was concerned that this story might not "bear the weight" because of its farcical nature (*Collected* 939). Yet to some, O'Connor's message is clear: Ruby is a pitiful example of what the sin of selfishness effects within the sacrament of marriage. As John R. May writes:

> Inasmuch as Ruby already has less life in herself through self-indulgence before the advent of her first child than her mother did after eight, the story strongly suggests that one gets "deader" by preventing life than by giving it.[6]

---

[5]Thomas Fawcett, *The Symbolic Language of Religion: An Introductory Study* (London: SCM Press Ltd., 1970) 139.

[6]May, *The Pruning Word*, 73.

O'Connor's belief in the Catholic position opposing birth control is corroborated in her letter to Cecil Dawkins in December of 1959:

> What the Church has decided definitely on matters of faith and morals, all Catholics must accept. . . . On matters of policy you may disagree, or on matters of opinion. You do not have to accept everything your particular pastor says unless it is something that is accepted by the whole Church, i.e., defined or canon law. . . .
>
> The Church has always been mindful of the relation between spirit and flesh; this has shown up in her definitions of the double nature of Christ, as well as in her care for what may seem to us to have nothing to do with religion—such as contraception. The Church is all of a piece. Her prohibition against the frustration of the marriage act has its true center perhaps in the doctrine of the resurrection of the body. This again is a *spiritual* doctrine, and beyond our comprehension. The Church doesn't say what this body will look like, but the doctrine proclaims the value of what is least about us, our flesh. . . .
>
> The Catholic can't think of birth control in relation to expediency but in relation to the nature of man under God. He has to find another solution to the population problem. (*HB* 365-66)

For readers familiar with O'Connor's explanations, "A Stroke of Good Fortune" does, indeed, justify a condemnation of Ruby in terms consistent with Catholic belief. Bill Hill's "slip up" provides the catalyst to compel Ruby to an adherence to the Catholic meaning of marriage, procreation. Readers would have little trouble interpreting Ruby's tacit agreement to interfere with the life-giving potential of the sexual act as a deliberate flaunting of the Catholic rules concerning birth control that places Ruby's soul in spiritual jeopardy. Additionally, Catholic readers would understand Ruby's unwillingness to accept God's gift of life, once her pregnancy is acknowledged, as a perversion of marriage. One of the nuptial blessings the priest confers upon the bride and bridegroom during the Catholic wedding ceremony underscores the meaning of this sacrament:

> Be appeased, O Lord, by our humble prayers, and in Your kindness assist this institution of marriage which You have ordained for the

> propagation of the human race; so that this union made here, joined by Your authority, may be preserved by Your help.[7]

Yet, internal conflicts within the story open it up to a very different reading. O'Connor's presentation of Ruby's fears is so evocative that she may be more due our compassion than our condemnation. The "it" O'Connor uses in reference to Ruby's unborn baby may only reflect Ruby's disassociation from her child, but it may also raise a caution in determining O'Connor's judgment of Ruby. O'Connor's unusual images of a menacing "it" waiting to destroy Ruby as her mother was destroyed, the imagery of a fetus as monster, the portrayal of Hartley Gilfeet as the horrific embodiment of the fetus his surname is meant to conjure up, and the suggestion that God lurks in ambush to capture unwilling subjects, are frightening ones. This macabre view of the new life within Ruby as a dark, hollow, mole-colored existence moving further and further down the staircase toward hell is not commonly embraced as either a modern Catholic or Christian belief and is what O'Connor means to condemn. But if Ruby is so in conflict with the rules and regulations of the Catholic Church that she desecrates the Sacrament of Marriage, she should be soundly punished or at the very least left painfully aware of her digressions. Yet, the evocation of fear and dismay at an unwanted pregnancy by a woman with an unhappy childhood is more in evidence in this story than any doctrinal condemnation.

According to Catholic doctrine, Ruby must repent and change if she is to be absolved from her sins, but readers expecting a Catholic solution to Ruby's past or present digressions find none. The problem in perceiving this as a Catholic story is precisely that Ruby never stands condemned for holding ideas contrary to Catholic teachings. As Gentry writes: "Ruby finally senses that she is part of the community of physical bodies, but this realization is forced upon her against her will."[8] O'Connor never teaches her the supreme lesson for her deviations from Catholic teaching. This O'Connor story does not instruct us about how a Catholic wife should behave in a proper Catholic marriage; it shows us a frightened woman forced into precisely the terrifying hole she wanted to escape. She is coerced into her bondage with procreation, not moved

[7]Hoever, *Saint Joseph Daily Missal*, 599.

[8]Gentry, *Flannery O'Connor's Religion of the Grotesque*, 94.

through revelation. The reader is left, as Ruby is left, aware of her problem but with no change effected and no solution offered.

If Bill Hill is the husband who forces his wife into complying with God's plan, Claud in "Revelation" is the husband who spiritually abandons his wife. Throughout this story Claud remains inattentive to his wife's innermost concerns. If he is not in the way of Mrs. Turpin's salvation, neither is he part of it, perhaps not even aware of it. In "Revelation," Mrs. Turpin's marriage, like her life, appears to be in control. But from the beginning of the story, Claud is a passive nonentity who is "accustomed to doing what she told him" (*CS* 488). Claud sighs and grins, but says nothing at all for the first eight and a half pages of the story, and little after that. He seems present only for Mrs. Turpin's amusement and to serve as a mirror reflecting her self-image. When he tells a racial joke that causes laughter in the doctor's office, Mrs. Turpin thanks God for her life, contemplating that "somebody else could have got Claud" (*CS* 499). She calls out to him when he's hurt in the doctor's office; she includes him in her vision of the procession to heaven. Yet, Claud never really reciprocates her concern. When she is attacked in the doctor's office, he does yell out "'Whoa!'" (*CS* 499). But after this he "crumpled and fell out of sight" (*CS* 499).

O'Connor intends the book-throwing incident by Mary Grace to propel Mrs. Turpin toward salvation. Mrs. Turpin's encounter with her moment of grace does shake her profoundly leaving her in extreme emotional distress after the episode. Yet, Mrs. Turpin is unable to confide her anguish to Claud despite her need for solace, because "He did not think of anything. He just went his way" (*CS* 502). O'Connor later indicates that, in fact, he "paid no attention to her humors" (*CS* 506). Claud not only does not think of anything; he does not think of nor pay any attention to his wife. Mrs. Turpin does ask him to kiss her, which he does, but he remains oblivious to her pain. "Her expression of ferocious concentration" makes no impression on him, and he leaves their bedroom while "She continued to study the ceiling" (*CS* 503).

Mrs. Turpin so needs to talk to someone to unburden herself of the force of Mary Grace's verbal assault that she is compelled to confide in the black women that she employs that she has been called "an old wart hog from hell" (*CS* 505). She receives no satisfaction from her disclosure and is never able to unburden herself to Claud, who remains divorced from her emotionally. Claud's shallowness and his remoteness from his wife correlate positively with O'Connor's language that minimizes the togetherness presupposed as a necessity in the Catholic idea of marriage. In fact, in this story, the union of these two people is only mentioned twice, and then with little focus. The first sentence of the story as they enter the doctor's office reads:

> The doctor's waiting room, which was very small, was almost full when the Turpins entered and Mrs. Turpin, who was very large, made it look even smaller by her presence. (*CS* 488)

The only other mention of them as a married couple occurs as they leave the doctor's office. This sentence reads: "Claud came limping out and the Turpins went home" (*CS* 502). "The Turpins" becomes only an amorphous plural term. Claud and Mrs. Turpin share a home, not a life. Mrs. Turpin's spouse is not part of her salvation, and her marriage assumes no sacramental meaning.

O'Connor's "ideal marriage" is apparently the violent wedding of Parker and Sarah Ruth in "Parker's Back." In many respects, Sarah Ruth exhibits the proper behavior for a bride as determined by one of the prayers offered during the Catholic Wedding Mass that states:

> Let the author of sin work none of his evil deeds within her; let her ever keep the Faith and the Commandments. Let her be true to one wedlock and shun all sinful embraces; let her strengthen weakness by stern discipline. Let her be grave in demeanor, honorable for her modesty, learned in heavenly doctrine, fruitful in children.[9]

Sarah Ruth certainly attempts to strengthen Parker's weaknesses by stern discipline, but their marriage gives a new and truly appalling meaning to her role as an "inseparable helpmate," a term that occurs in the introductory part of the above prayer.[10]

In the opening paragraph of "Parker's Back," Parker reflects on his marriage and his wife, wonders "why he stayed with her," and feels ashamed that he has (*CS* 510). In the first paragraph O'Connor uses the adjectives *plain, thin, drawn, tight, gray, sharp, pregnant* to describe Sarah Ruth. Her skin is like an onion's and her eyes "like the points of

[9]Hoever, *Saint Joseph Daily Missal*, 600.
[10]Ibid., 599.

two icepicks"; she is not an attractive nor loveable mate even in Parker's eyes, yet he finds himself strongly attracted to her (*CS* 510).

The story continues in its ironic vein when it states that "In addition to her other bad qualities, she was forever sniffing up sin" (*CS* 510). It is precisely Sarah Ruth's hounddog talents that make her a valued mate in O'Connor's eyes. O'Connor writes that Parker

> had a suspicion that she actually liked everything she said she didn't. He could account for her one way or another; it was himself he could not understand. (*CS* 510)

Parker is obsessed with Sarah Ruth, whom O'Connor intends as an instrument of salvation. Sarah Ruth will perform for him the necessary violence needed to bring him to his senses and to his God. From the time Parker returns home with "the haloed head of a flat stern Byzantine Christ with all-demanding eyes" tattooed on his back, the verbs used in connection with Sarah Ruth portray her as a stern disciplinarian:

> Sarah Ruth loomed there . . .
>
> she demanded . . .
>
> Sarah Ruth growled . . .
>
> Sarah Ruth screamed . . .
>
> she grabbed up the broom and began to thrash him . . .
>
> she had nearly knocked him senseless . . .
>
> She stamped the broom . . .
>
> her eyes hardened. (*CS* 522; 528; 529; 530)

Brian Ragen in *A Wreck on the Road to Damascus: Innocence, Guilt, & Conversion in Flannery O'Connor* sees Sarah Ruth as Parker's "savior":

> And it is Sarah Ruth who completes Parker's moment of grace by rejecting him and wounding his back. Thanks to that rejection, and thus to the marriage that allows it, Parker participates in the sufferings of Christ. The marriage, in a strange way, has been a channel of grace at least for Parker.[11]

Yet the strangeness of this marital union allows room for misinterpretation. Those approaching this story with a Catholic or Christian idea of marriage, which views such an alliance as a partnership joined in love, most probably would not want to trade places with Parker who "sat there and let her beat him until she had nearly knocked him senseless and large welts had formed on the face of the tattooed Christ" (*CS* 529). O'Connor depicts Parker as an errant soul who must be beaten into spiritual awareness. Only the violent righteousness of Sarah Ruth can hurl him onto the path toward salvation.

To the Christian love of God and love between people are fundamental precepts. Catholics are commanded to obey the Ten Commandments, which require love of God, family, and neighbor. Love is additionally important to Catholics as it is defined by the philosophy set forth in the Golden Rule, the "guiding rule of humanism," proclaimed by Christ at the Last Supper when he asked that his followers "Love one another."[12] In a 15 September 1955 letter to "A," O'Connor stressed her belief in the importance of love: "the mystery of the Redemption and our salvation is worked out on earth according as we love one another" (*HB* 102). However, love in any of its familiar definitions is distinctly absent from Flannery O'Connor's works. In particular, in O'Connor's fiction, filial duty as commanded by God in the Commandment "Honor thy father and thy mother" encompasses neither love as might be presumed by a modern explication, nor respect as might be assumed by an older, more traditional interpretation.

Family life in "Greenleaf" seems to be defined by malice more than by what is traditionally recognized as either love or respect. Mrs. May is ashamed of her sons Wesley and Scofield. "Scofield only exasperated her beyond endurance but Wesley caused her real anxiety," an anxiety caused not by concern for his well-being, but rather from embarrassment at his

---

[11]Brian Ragen, *A Wreck on the Road to Damascus: Innocence, Guilt, & Conversion in Flannery O'Connor* (Chicago: Loyola University Press, 1989) 53.

[12]Deedy, *The Catholic Fact Book*, 103-104.

behavior (*CS* 319). In return neither Wesley nor Scofield love their mother. Scofield looks at her "wickedly" and mockingly calls her "Sugar-pie" while menacingly showing her an "exaggerated expanse of teeth" (*CS* 320). Her response to this gesture of meanness in her house with neither love nor honor is a cold look. Both motherly love, as usually represented, and filial consideration, as generally expected, are decidedly absent here.

O'Connor's fictional adventure in familial malevolence continues as both boys deliberately aggravate Mrs. May. O'Connor describes their interactions as "teas[ing]." But the connotation of "teased" is too playful for the malice found in this relationship. The ensuing dialogue (I have edited out "she said," etc.) between mother and sons exhibits the enmity that exists in this family:

> [*Mrs. May*]: I'm the victim. I've always been the victim.
>
> [*Wesley*]: Pass the butter to the victim.
>
> [*Scofield*]: Why Mamma, ain't you ashamed to shoot an old bull that ain't done nothing but give you a little scrub strain in your herd? I declare . . . with the Mamma I got it's a wonder I turned out to be such a nice boy!
>
> [*Wesley*]: You ain't her boy, Son.
>
> [*Scofield*]: All I know is . . . I done mighty well to be as nice as I am seeing what I come from. (*CS* 327)

Perhaps O'Connor used the word "teased" to describe this repartee for what she might consider comic effect. However, this family scene is full of emotional violence as O'Connor makes clear with the authorial comment: "but Wesley made his own particular tone come through it like a knife edge" as he confronts his brother (*CS* 327). This exchange of sarcasm ends with O'Connor's noting "an ugly family resemblance" between the two brothers, Scofield's comment to Wesley that "Nobody feels sorry for a lousy bastard like you," and "a crash of dishes" as the brothers come to blows (*CS* 327). Undoubtedly, O'Connor intends this family relationship to indicate what "love" becomes among the lost. Mrs. May has not raised her boys with religion as has Mrs. Greenleaf. She has been concerned with life's practicalities and has actually spurned the religious practices of the fanatic Mrs. Greenleaf by telling her to stop her praying and "'go wash your children's clothes!'" (*CS* 317). It is Mrs. Greenleaf's boys who "had advanced in the world" and not her own (*CS* 317). Whatever makes Mrs. Greenleaf a loving mother, other than her fundamentalist beliefs, is not presented in the story, however, leaving O'Connor's world charged with the presence of hatred instead of love in the family life she explores.

Critics have come to varying conclusions about O'Connor's sense of family. May writes that in "A Good Man Is Hard to Find"

> Even Bailey had shown sign of filial piety under the threat of death; the man who had just cursed his mother for identifying The Misfit said affectionately as he left for the wood, "I'll be back in a minute, Mamma, wait on me!"[13]

Throughout the story, Bailey has shown no affection for his mother. When she asked him to dance at Red Sammy's "he only glared at her" (*CS* 121). After the accident, the grandmother who had previously contemplated Bailey's lack of her "naturally sunny disposition" wished she were "injured so that Bailey's wrath would not come down on her all at once" (*CS* 121; 125). And the curse that he hurls at his mother when she foolishly verbalizes her recognition of The Misfit "shocked even the children" (*CS* 127). O'Connor perhaps means to equate Bailey's last statement to his mother with his mother's last tender touch extended to The Misfit. Presumably, Bailey would have been a good man if there was someone there to shoot *him* every moment also.

This same scenario of last minute love is repeated with Julian and his mother in "Everything That Rises Must Converge." Julian, who has spent the entire story feeling "an evil urge to break her spirit," is suddenly infused with feelings of love and tenderness for his mother as she lies fallen on the ground in her death throes from a stroke (*CS* 409). Julian cries out in fright at her impending death: "Darling, sweetheart, wait!" while he desperately seeks help (*CS* 420). Only when there can be no reciprocity nor even mutual acknowledgement of his "love" for his mother, and only then, does O'Connor have Julian indicate his "filial piety."

---

[13]May, *The Pruning Word*, 63-64.

Marshall Bruce Gentry considers that

> Julian's "return" to his mother can be only a temporary postponement. . . . Never again will he have his mother's falsely aristocratic stance to depend upon to serve him as the convenient, secure object of his mental ridicule and self-justification. In the story his false spiritual and intellectual haven from history has been destroyed, though of course he is still free to fantasize another escapist haven.[14]

Julian's mother is never represented as an object of "love" to Julian. She merely represents the occasion for his own bad temper and the shield to his insecurities. His agony at her death is not due to loss of her as a mother-figure, but rather to the collapse of his own elitist fantasies.

O'Connor's idea of the good mother resembles her idea of the good wife. Proper motherly love is that which drives the child to God. In *Wise Blood* Haze Motes's family life is rather unorthodox but instrumental in leading him to seek God. When accompanying his father to a carnival as a small child, Haze followed him to a sideshow and saw a sexually suggestive woman. O'Connor's description of Haze's mother after this incident associates her with his consciousness of sin. Frightened after his experience Haze sees that

> His mother was standing by the washpot in the yard, looking at him, when he got home. She wore black all the time and her dresses were longer than other women's. . . . She had a cross-shaped face and hair pulled close to her head. (*Collected* 35)

Haze's mother offers no comfort to her son, but rather makes him feel guilty and sinful for having been a witness to the carnival's freak show. She "hit him across the legs with the stick," saying "'Jesus died to redeem you'" (*Collected* 36). O'Connor connects Haze's mother with her "cross-shaped face" to the Redeemer, and she teaches Haze the "right" lessons. These carefully selected images create a picture linking her austerity and retribution to the saving power of the cross, and in O'Connor's terms she is the kind of mother who will save the children of a degenerate society.

---

[14]Gentry, *Flannery O'Connor's Religion of the Grotesque*, 71.

Haze's experience with his preacher-grandfather extends the idea of God's design in family love. As Haze remembers his early years filled with the sober, reproving religion of his grandfather, he illustrates what O'Connor views as the religious oversight incumbent upon family authority figures if their offspring are to be saved:

> The old man would point to his grandson, Haze. He had a particular disrespect for him because his own face was repeated almost exactly in the child's and seemed to mock him. (*Collected* 11)

Haze's recollections of his grandfather as preacher to the crowds that gathered in Eastrod include remembering the question he heard posed about himself:

> Did they know that even for that boy there, for that mean sinful unthinking boy standing there with his dirty hands clenching and unclenching at his sides, Jesus would die ten million deaths before He would let him lose his soul? (*Collected* 11)

O'Connor repeatedly reinforces the message that harsh, chiding behavior on the part of parental figures is the only means of assuring salvation. And Haze's family does possess these characteristics. However, as fictional representations of family models and authority figures, Haze's mother and his grandfather are more likely grotesque images of ignorance, bias, and brutality than of familial love.

O'Connor's ironic sense of humor casts her most perverse distortion of the mother-figure in the tender, cradling madonna role she assigns to Sabbath Lily Hawks later on in the novel. When Sabbath Lily, who never knew her own mother, approaches Haze with Enoch Emery's stolen shrunken museum mummy cradled in her arms, she is clearly a blasphemous distortion of the madonna with child. The mummy's "head fitted exactly into the hollow of her shoulder" and she says to Haze "'Call me Momma now'" (*Collected* 104; 106). Although Sabbath Lily is the secular world's mockery of the mother of God, she is sincere, gentle, and ultimately pathetic in this vision of her "motherhood." Haze becomes infuriated at her blasphemy on the Holy Family when she refers to him as the mummy's "daddy" and his hand

> lunged and snatched the shriveled body and threw it against the wall. The head popped and the trash inside sprayed out in a little cloud of dust. (*Collected* 106)

Once again O'Connor distances Haze's actions from Haze as person (his hand performs the action) to detach further his relationship to this "family."[15] The images of horror continue:

> Haze snatched the skin off the floor. He opened the outside door where the landlady thought there had once been a fire-escape, and flung out what he had in his hand. (*Collected* 106)

Haze must remove the offending "baby" and the "trash" he signifies. He hurls the mummy out the window as repudiation of this sacrilegious portrayal. O'Connor sees Haze's response as evidence of the essential reverence he has for God and the Holy Family.

Although O'Connor's doctrinal objectives legitimize Haze's rejection of the empty, hollow body of the mummy-child as well as his rejection of the empty, spiritually hollow Sabbath Lily as evidence of proper Christian reverence, the family associations in this novel are inconsistent with Christian values. It is only with Haze's mock family that O'Connor associates images of love and closeness. Sabbath Lily, the counter-madonna, cradles the mummy-child tenderly in her arms:

> Some of his hair had come undone and she brushed it back where it belonged, holding him in the crook of her arm and looking down into his squinched face. . . . She began to rock him a little in her arm and a slight reflection of the same grin appeared on her own face. "Well I declare," she murmured, "you're right cute, ain't you?" (*Collected* 104)

Nowhere in the entire novel does O'Connor present images of a desirable earthly or heavenly family or of a recognizable love that might exist among such family members. Her only familial portrayals require constant readjustments in the reader's assessment of love and family. The reader who has been repulsed by O'Connor's depictions of Haze's real

---

[15]See chapter 1 for further discussion of using bodily parts as characters.

family may be more confused by the gestures of maternal love in the image of the young girl and her mummy-child.

Lewis Lawson's assessment of *Wise Blood* is that O'Connor's "Extremely incongruous images . . . convince us that here indeed is a strange new world. . . . It is indeed a warped world, one which has been likened to a Chagall painting."[16] Lawson feels that O'Connor "would not have departed from the conventional structure and treatment of the novel, if she had thought innovations in style or absurdities in content would detract from her vision," but the failure of readers to read her meaning suggests that her innovations, indeed, may have produced effects she did not foresee.[17]

After an acquaintance with O'Connor's letters and lectures one comes to realize that women such as Haze's mother and Sarah Ruth, who either beat their children into singlemindedly pursuing redemption, or who soundly thrash their husbands into recognizing the one true God, are not in O'Connor's mind unpossessed of love, but rather their love of God is more compelling than any earthly manifestations. In O'Connor's estimation, stern, humorless, fanatically religious, God-demanding women are necessary to whip their children or husbands into godliness. Women such as Mrs. Greenleaf, Haze's mother, and Sarah Ruth are indispensable and are the models O'Connor intends to be emulated if children and husbands are ever to know the one true God and attain salvation. But these images do not readily coincide with the values taught by Christian religions that are masculinist in orientation, not feminist or womanly. O'Connor's family representations become a reversal of the traditional '50s and '60s roles of female as loving nurturer and male as ultimate disciplinarian.

Familial relationships such as the ones Haze is subjected to (a grandfather who preaches hell-fire, a father who exposes him to it, and a mother who is intent on making it his reality) would perhaps more likely produce a child emotionally scarred and incapable of love. Marriages that isolate and demean through emotional neglect and physical battering open the door to the divorce court or the jailhouse more than they might to the gates of heaven. Readers are distracted from O'Connor's Catholic vision by her hateful and horror-invoking images and language choices that inadequately balance the emblematic intent of the

---

[16]Lewis A. Lawson, "The Perfect Deformity: *Wise Blood*," *Renascence: Essays on Values in Literature* 17/2 (Spring 1965): 37.

[17]Ibid., 38.

stories with the social reality of a specific world in which she sets them. In doctrine, the stories depend on the Incarnation, but the God evoked by O'Connor's language is the God of Wrath of the Old Testament. Christ, the Lamb of God, appears only in mock-ups such as Sabbath Lily's that drain the image of its power. Nowhere does the love of Christ itself touch the lives of the characters as "love." The consistently demeaning portrait of humanity O'Connor gives us may well require a miracle of Grace for their souls to be redeemed, but measuring out the fates of these characters with fear and punishment will leave little evidence that their God is one of love and mercy.

5.
The Grammar of Negation

O'Connor was convinced that the world surrounding her had actively rejected belief in divine authority. To represent this world accurately, she felt compelled to portray the negativism she perceived as a factually accurate appraisal of contemporary humanity. She writes an explanation to "A" in 1955 about the negativism prevalent in her fiction: "Another reason for the negative appearance: if you live today you breathe in nihilism" (*HB* 97). George L. Dillon writes about the grammatical implications of negatives:

> Perhaps the first point about a negative is that it negates an expectation. Although something is said not to be the case, it might have been: to comprehend it, then, we must see the expectation that is negated as a plausible one, an outgrowth of possibilities inherent in the world at that point.[1]

The appearance of negatives in O'Connor's stories extends beyond her themes and character portrayals to yield an all pervasive negative quality that seems to deny her fictional characters the fate that might have been. In her negative world only the offer of grace can effect change. However, O'Connor's negative language accentuates a corresponding spiritual environment from which escape seems impossible.

Through grammatical structures and word play O'Connor encases her characters in a language that denies them the possibilities of attaining the salvation toward which they struggle. Further, this negativism does not cease once the moment of grace is offered. O'Connor's skill at veiling her fictional message is part of her skill as a writer; however, the unveiling of her grammatical structures raises questions as to the ultimate destiny her characters achieve. An underlying negativism emphasizes the warning intended for her reading public, but the fact that negatives continue to plague her characters after they receive a glimpse of salvation blurs the essence of her message, and perhaps even denies her characters the fate she would choose for them. To see beyond the negative appearance and reach the conclusions O'Connor wished us to reach

---

[1]George L. Dillon, *Language Processing and the Reading of Literature: Toward a Modal of Comprehension* (Bloomington: Indiana University Press, 1978) 142.

requires a familiarity with her private correspondence and lectures. Part of the problem in reaching the conclusions O'Connor intended is that in O'Connor's stories denotations are often obscured by more familiar and more readily available connotations.

Negative structures are undeniably observable in "Good Country People." From the moment Hulga sets out to meet the Bible salesman until the end of the story, fifty-six paragraphs with a total of 204 sentences occur (*CS* 284-91). Negative words or negative verbs appear in forty-four of these paragraphs (79%); only twelve paragraphs (21%) have a positive cast, a condition that gives this passage an overwhelmingly negative complexion. Additionally, eighty-eight of the 204 total sentences within these fifty-six paragraphs (43%) express negativity. To complement her negative verb constructions, in this same section of the story, O'Connor also uses the following words (with the frequencies of use indicated) that further enhance the negativistic atmosphere:

WORDS	FREQUENCY
1. but	21
2. nothing	7
3. no	7
4. without	5
5. never	4
6. disappeared	2
7. no one	2
8. none	2
9. remove[d]	2
10. hollow	2

The predominance of the negative coordinate conjunction "but" in this story subtly implies an environment where exceptions or contradictions flourish. The plethora of words that obliterate existence or disguise its reality gives evidence of a world where despair seems almost tangible. Additional words in this section with negative connotations or with implications of concealment that work to negate expectations are:

> illusions, nowhere, empty, blindfolds, losing, escaping, detached, distance, destroy, surrendering, escaping, forgetting, doubted, abashed, unusual, unexceptional, uncertain, blankly, mesmerized, different.

The tension created in O'Connor's language by this negative overtone tempers any glimmer of hope that might exist for the spiritual future of her characters by offering disputable and confounding testimony as surrounding accompaniments when these characters are offered views of their final visions.

While it is possible to assume that O'Connor meant to indicate negativity about the world in which her godless characters live, and especially about the world surrounding Hulga, the epitome of nihilism, she provides no relief for Hulga once she has been exposed to God's grace. Though Hulga is shattered by her experiences, O'Connor offers her no release from negation. As the story ends, Hulga "was left" with a "churning face." The verb "was left" indicates her passive condition; the active loss of her leg dictates that Hulga was *not* able to go anywhere as she contemplates the reality that now surrounds her.

In contrast, Hulga sees the Bible salesman "struggling successfully over the green speckled lake" (*CS* 291). One might expect that he would "struggle," for the Bible salesman is the obvious villain and a connection with negatives would be appropriate. Yet, the Bible salesman, by an alliance with the adverb "successfully," can somehow escape negativity. The ironic image O'Connor leaves with her readers is that the Bible salesman, as evil manifest, walks the green earth in a metaphor reminiscent of Jesus, God Incarnate, walking on the waters. Like Jesus, the Bible salesman accomplishes this action in triumph. Hulga, whom the reader might expect to be redeemed after her sudden realization, is left prostrate, overcome not only by her nihilism but even more importantly thoroughly incapacitated by the language of negativity that obfuscates her chances for redemption.

"A Temple of the Holy Ghost" has been described as "one of O'Connor's most positive and reassuring pictures of human potentiality" and initially appears unlike the despairing portrait of humanity sketched in "Good Country People."[2] The unnamed child in the story does seem to achieve a sort of humility when she considers, in one of her many reveries, that of her numerous faults she "was eaten up . . . with the sin of Pride, the worst one" (*CS* 243). However, once the child begins to acknowledge her part in God's scheme, her language is burdened with negatives. O'Connor expresses her prayer in the following passage:

---

[2]May, *The Pruning Word*, 74.

> Hep me not to be so mean, she began mechanically. Hep me not to give her so much sass. Hep me not to talk like I do. Her mind began to get quiet and then empty but when the priest raised the monstrance with the Host shining ivory-colored in the center of it, she was thinking of the tent at the fair that had the freak in it. (*CS* 247-48)

Every one of these sentences expresses a negative intent. Perhaps O'Connor means to suggest the child's preparation for God's revelation through her entrance into the traditional Christian *Via Negativa.*

O'Connor explicitly indicates in several instances that the child "didn't have anything she could think of," that she was "empty-minded" (*CS* 244). Her final prayer even emphasizes that "Her mind began to get quiet and then empty" (*CS* 248). This emptying seems to allow for her eventual salvation through her spiritual entrance into mysticism. As Alain Cugno explains,

> mysticism is negative, because it contrasts believing (which derives from faith) with seeing. For mysticism, what shall ultimately be seen is the same as what is now believed. But in relation to seeing, believing is negative. We do not see what we believe.[3]

Eugene A. Maio, discusses the view the mystic must attain to reach God:

> God, one and simple, is beyond the visible universe. If God cannot be experienced within the human, finite condition, then the only recourse is to escape the human condition, to voluntarily undertake a journey through a night in which all that is not God is abandoned.[4]

As Maio reveals, the philosophy of St. John of the Cross embodies the belief that "The journey to God must therefore be a *negative way*: a denial, a disengagement, an annihilation of everything that is not God."[5] Yet confusion surrounds the child's spiritual condition. The problem of interpreting the child's thought as approaching the philosophy of mystics such as St. John of the Cross is exemplified in the language that O'Con-

---

[3]Alain Cugno, *Saint John of the Cross: The Life and Thought of Christian Mystic* (London: Burns & Oates, 1979) 16.

[4]Eugene A. Maio, *St. John of the Cross: The Imagery of Eros* (Madrid: Playor, S.A., 1973) 163.

[5]Ibid., 164.

nor chooses for the child. In her prayer, the child does seem to be using negatives to effect a positive change and might even be considered as contemplating negation to achieve sanctification. In the first three sentences of her prayer, the negativism is overtly expressed in the negative "not." However, the curious aspect of this "prayer" the child offers to God is contained in the intensifiers "so" and "like." The child only asks God if she could "not . . . be *so* mean," "not . . . give . . . *so much* sass," "not . . . talk *like I do*." Although the negatives in the passage can be considered as evidence of the child's humility and her submissiveness in the face of God, her use of the intensifiers quantifies the degree to which she will accept change. Her request of God reinforces her clinging adherence to her previously detailed mean-spirited disposition. She will continue her misbehavior; only the degree of her misconduct will be mitigated.

The use of the words "so" and "so much" indicates that the child is unwilling to pray for a complete conduct change. She is unwilling to reach the totality of negation in which "*all* that is not God is abandoned." When she asks if she might not talk "like I do" the implication is that the ill manner in which she talks is an intricate and inextricable part of her personality and is something she is reluctant to eliminate completely. O'Connor's use of these intensifiers only allows for a degree of change, not the "total and uncompromising" posture that St. John of the Cross in *Ascent of Mount Carmel* felt necessary to ensure that one's "soul may receive the likeness of God."[6]

As the child contemplates her future she feels that

> She would have to be a saint because that was the occupation that included everything you could know; and yet she knew she would never be a saint. She did not steal or murder but she was a born liar and slothful and she sassed her mother and was deliberately ugly to almost everybody. (*CS* 243)

O'Connor's language in this passage emphasizes the inherency of the child's meanness when she calls her a "born liar" whose ugliness is "deliberate." The positive note in this story becomes entangled and overtaken by the language of negativity. The child, through her prayer, concedes her imperfections but consents only to remain in a modifying position. Her

---

[6]Ibid.

mechanical prayer, clouded by thoughts of the freak at the fair, unites her with the freak's acceptance of his condition. She, like the freak, does not "'dispute hit. This is the way He wanted me to be'" (*CS* 248). She approaches the negative way to salvation, but deliberately, through linguistic choices, stops short of the total negativity needed to empty her soul of "everything that is not God."

The last image the reader has of the child as she leaves the religious setting of the convent is of

> the big nun [who] swooped down on her mischievously and nearly smothered her in the black habit, mashing the side of her face into the crucifix hitched onto her belt and then holding her off and looking at her with little periwinkle eyes. (*CS* 248)

The child herself is "nearly smothered" into the blackness of the nun's clothing, her face "mashing" the crucifix, yet she is deprived of a complete religious union. The child, through her non-prayer, has spiritually negated a change in deportment. O'Connor's language, which intimately but negatively associates the child with the personages or articles of religion, combine with the child's deliberate behavior to suggest her non-redemption. Therefore, while May writes that "the child comes—as each of us must—to realize what her limitations are but more importantly, what she can accomplish despite them," the negative language of the child and the smothering, hurtful images that intimately connect her to the people and objects important to her religion, and by implication her salvation, "dispute hit."[7] O'Connor's language of negation leaves the child unable to articulate "what she can accomplish despite" her limitations. She is obsessed, instead, with her frailties and unconscious of her possibilities. Her mind never becomes "empty" enough to receive God's grace. The underlying restrictions placed on her through her grammatical choices, as well as the injurious union with the nun and crucifix, obscure the possibility of an optimistic spiritual outcome for the child, shutting her out of any religious fulfillment.

Because she was concerned that her message not be transparent, O'Connor employed other linguistic techniques that operate in tandem with her language of negation. She made every effort to prevent her intentions from appearing obvious by embedding meaning deeply within

[7]May, *The Pruning Word*, 76.

the story's fibre, using a variety of artistic tactics. As she stated in *Mystery and Manners*:

> When you can state the theme of a story, when you can separate it from the story itself, then you can be sure the story is not a very good one. The meaning of a story has to be embodied in it, has to be made concrete in it. (*MM* 96)

Concealing within the names of characters coded meanings that challenge the reader to levels of verbal cleverness that themselves become questionable is one method O'Connor utilized to secure redemptive ambiguity for her characters. For example, her use of names may actually involve extended jokes, or symbols, or authorial playfulness in an attempt to amplify mystery within the her stories.

Robert Fitzgerald writes that "Hoover Shoates" [sic] was "a name we all celebrated," an indication that names are obviously important to O'Connor's style although not in the usual sense.[8] And Sally Fitzgerald writes that "The world of the absurd delighted her. She regaled us with . . . birth announcements of infants with names that had to be read to be believed" (*HB* xiii). Names provide O'Connor with another means of disguising her artistic intent and work as mysterious complements to her linguistic negativity. Edward Kessler suggests that the reader of O'Connor's fiction "must question and continually reexamine gestures, both physical and verbal, in order to approach the hidden truth they so often misrepresent."[9] Kessler's comment may be extended beyond gestures to cover O'Connor's use of anagram as a cryptic linguistic naming tool. Joy-Hulga's name change in "Good Country People" becomes on one level a sign that she would replace God's joy with her self-appointed nihilism. But, the verbal play may not stop there. O'Connor makes a point of emphasizing that Joy triumphantly created a new identity for herself by legally changing her name to Hulga. O'Connor stresses Joy-Hulga's naming as a "creative act" when she writes that Joy-Hulga

---

[8]Robert Fitzgerald, introduction, *Everything that Rises Must Converge*, xv. See Chapter 1 for a discussion of other naming strategies.

[9]Kessler, *Flannery O'Connor and the Language of the Apocalypse,* 49.

> had a vision of the name working like the ugly sweating Vulcan who stayed in the furnace and to whom, presumably, the goddess had to come when called. (*CS* 275)

However, the name "Hulga" also surreptitiously emerges as an anagram for the word "laugh."[10] And, thus, while Joy's "creative act" appears to have displaced a prior identity connected with the emotion of "joy," her new name indeed conceals the word "laugh," which itself is the overt expression of "joy." O'Connor's use of the anagram "Hulga" must engender anew speculations about this character's fate.

The layered connection of joy to laugh as contained in the "Joy-Hulga" name change raises questions about what, if any, transformation Joy effected when she became Hulga. The name "Hulga" with its clandestine relationship to "laugh" reestablishes an intimate association with this character's previous identity, "Joy," and questions whether she, as character, is capable of any change at all. Is the change to "Hulga" merely cosmetic, allowing her to remain covertly "Joy"?

Additionally, recognition of the name "Hulga," as an anagram for "laugh" secretly invalidates Hulga's contention that she has destroyed her previous identity by a "creative act":

> One of her major triumphs was that her mother had not been able to turn her dust into Joy, but the greater one was that she had been able to turn it herself into Hulga. (*CS* 275)

If destruction does indeed spawn creation, as Joy-Hulga believes occurred with her legal name change, then the Bible salesman's destruction of Hulga could be interpreted as once again destroying her assumed identity, encompassed in the name "Hulga," to recreate "laugh," the outcome of "Joy." The destruction of the former would thus beget the latter, returning her to her former existence. Despite her attempt at nihilistic cleverness, Hulga has accomplished nothing and triumph is nonexistent. Her name still intimately connects her to the literal consequences of joy.

The Hulga who appears at the end of the story remains shrouded in mystery. Is she still in possession of her previous reality, which would leave her without hope for salvation? Has she, in fact, received Grace,

---

[10]I am indebted to Dr. Sarah Liggett, Associate Professor of English at Louisiana State University, for this insight.

which would indicate that no effort to transform herself into a nihilist can ever take the essential "Joy" out of her soul? Or does O'Connor intend that the Bible salesman's devastation of Hulga would strip her of both identities since his annihilating behavior would literally eradicate "Hulga" which by implication contains "Joy"? Is Hulga not only left with the "nothing" she has always believed in, but also rendered incapable of returning to "Joy"? Or was O'Connor's intention to rid Hulga of her "Joy" thereby leaving her soul salvable after all?

O'Connor preserves the integrity of this mystery when she discusses her concept of "joy" in a 1963 letter to Janet McKane. She comments that "joy, may be a redemptive experience itself and not just the fruit of one. Perhaps however joy is the outgrowth of suffering in a special way" (*HB* 527). O'Connor's masterful incorporation of mystery into Joy's name change, if it is deliberate, hints at her tremendous artistic control. Through anagram Joy-Hulga has been returned full circle into an existence neither she nor the Bible salesman seems capable of fully destroying or creating. Yet O'Connor's metaphor of mystery obscures a definitive solution. The reader must wonder if O'Connor intended Hulga's "destruction" to once again return her to a world where "a smile [of Joy] never hurt anyone" (*CS* 276). Or does O'Connor intend this character to echo her own words to her mother:

> "Woman! do you ever look inside? Do you ever look inside and see what you are *not*? God!" (*CS* 276)

"Hulga" seems not to be "Joy" nor "Joy" "Hulga," and the "laugh" may be with the clever reader.

A second instance of anagram in O'Connor's fictional happenings occurs in two O'Connor stories, "A Stroke of Good Fortune" and "The Lame Shall Enter First." In both of these stories O'Connor names a character "Rufus." In addition to the name's sound which may echo words such as "rue," and "rueful," meaning sorrow, regret, or remorse, the letters of the name "Rufus" when reversed become an anagram for "Sufur," a spelling aberration, but a phonetic pronunciation for "suffer." O'Connor reinforces this concept through additional associations with the idea of anguish and torment since the name "Rufus" has biblical implications that connect it with suffering. According to the Gospel of St. Mark, Rufus was the son of Simon of Cyrene who was compelled by the Romans to help Jesus carry his cross on the way to Calvary. *The Inter-*

national Standard Bible Encyclopaedia indicates that the apostle Paul greeted Rufus as "the chosen in the Lord" and that the name itself "meaning 'red,' 'reddish,' was . . . one of the commonest of slave names."[11] This association of Rufus as a son of one who shared Christ's sorrow, along with an additional connection to slavery, seems to substantiate the bond of sorrow and suffering related to this name and would conform as well with O'Connor's reliance on names as a means to sustain her fictional message. And perhaps, the connection of the names "Rufus" and "Ruby" to the color red through their resemblance to the words "rufescence" and "rubescence," both associated with redness, is yet another bond that unites these characters to Christ's suffering as manifested in the shedding of his sacred blood.

In "A Stroke of Good Fortune," Ruby continually indicates that Rufus, her "baby" brother, is the cause of much suffering. She has to cook collard greens for him, a vegetable that reminds her of her squalid past, and she is haunted by the memory of the night he was born to cause her mother misery. O'Connor has Ruby refer to Rufus as only "an enfant" when Laverne Watts, her neighbor, expresses a sexual interest in him. This association of Rufus with the colloquial spelling/pronunciation of "infant," illustrates O'Connor's playful orthographic reconstructions, and also foreshadows Ruby's thoughts of her unborn baby at the end of the story, which once again are linked with her "baby" brother. Ruby sees her unborn child "as if it were out nowhere in nothing, out nowhere, resting and waiting, with plenty of time" (*Collected* 196). This perception of the impact that her own baby will have on her is an echo of how Ruby perceived Rufus' birth affecting her mother: "All that misery for Rufus!" (*Collected* 186). Not only did each of her mother's children make her mother "deader," but Rufus, in particular, made her mother suffer as Ruby feels she will suffer with her own child. As O'Connor makes clear, Rufus was also "waiting out nowhere before he was born, just waiting, waiting to make his mother, only thirty-four, into an old woman" (*Collected* 186).

The reader must wonder if Ruby's suffering cleanses her from her sins and makes her worthy to receive God's grace. When Ruby finally makes her way to her friend Laverne's apartment, she is still unaware of

[11]James Orr, ed. *The International Standard Bible Encyclopaedia* (Grand Rapids MI: William B. Eerdmans Publishing Co., 1960) 4: 2625.

her pregnancy. There she is suddenly confronted with her impending motherhood as Laverne accurately assesses her condition. From this point on, Ruby states or thinks the following (frequencies of occurrence indicated):

STATEMENTS/THOUGHTS	FREQUENCIES
"Not me!"	3
"Oh no not me!"	1
"That ain't going to happen to me!"	1
"It is not!"	1
"I ain't going to have any baby!"	1
"No."/ "Nooo" / no	7
She was not . . .	2
it could not . . .	2
(*Collected* 193-96)	

Ruby's previous connection to suffering serves not as penance to free her from her sin of practicing birth control, a mortal sin in the eyes of the Catholic Church. Ruby never comes to terms with her pregnancy. She continues her negation and abject denial of her condition, refusing to accept God's will and the life she has miraculously been allowed to create. The story ends replete with negation as O'Connor reiterates the very words she had previously used to describe the suffering experienced by Ruby's mother because of her many pregnancies, but this time the anguish applies to and is centered around Ruby's unacceptance of her unborn who was also "out nowhere in nothing, out nowhere, resting and waiting with plenty of time" (*Collected* 196). Ruby feels afflicted not blessed. Can O'Connor's language allow us to see her as saved?

The Rufus in "The Lame Shall Enter First" experiences suffering as well as causes it. Sheppard details the deprivations and indignities Rufus Johnson has had to endure to his own child, Norton. Rufus eats out of garbage cans, he was in the reformatory, his father died, his mother is in prison, he "was raised by his grandfather in a shack without water or electricity and the old man beat him every day," he has a misshapen foot, and one leg is shorter than the other (*CS* 447). Rufus, however, is also the focal point around whom Sheppard's suffering pivots. Through Rufus's "teachings," Norton, Sheppard's only child, attempts to share in his mother's everlasting life, and thereby commits suicide so that he, too, might see heaven. Rufus, therefore, is instrumental in bringing the full realization of suffering to Sheppard. He is necessary to Sheppard's "moment of grace." At one point in the story, Sheppard says to Rufus "How about helping me out? Stay here for a while with us, Rufus. I need your help" (*CS* 457). Sheppard needs help in attaining salvation. He will be unable to realize his redemption without experiencing suffering and making atonement for his transgressions. Sheppard's cognizance of his own failings only surfaces with his discovery of the body of his only child hanging from the rafter in the attic. Norton's death, the beginning of Sheppard's sufferings, has been precipitated by Rufus, who is both the cause and the result of the verb "Sufur."

Character references throughout this story are further indications that O'Connor did intend "Rufus" as the embodiment of suffering. In this story whenever the narrator refers to this character, the surname "Johnson," and only "Johnson," is used. On the other hand, Sheppard, who must have an intimate connection with suffering in order potentially to merit salvation, refers to this character four times with his full name "Rufus Johnson" and the remainder of the time with only the first name, "Rufus." Norton, whose act of suicide will set Sheppard's suffering in motion, names this character twice, and both times he calls him "Rufus." Once when Rufus talks about going to hell when he dies, a frightened Norton fearing that his dead mother may be experiencing the everlasting punishment of hell asks the all important question: "'Is she there, Rufus?' he said. 'Is she there, burning up?'" (*CS* 462). And Norton uses the name "Rufus" once again in talking with this character: "'Repent, Rufus,' Norton said in a pleading voice. 'Repent, hear? You don't want to go to hell'" (*CS* 476). Both instances of Norton's naming are connected in his mind with hell, the place where souls stained with the tarnish of mortal sins are sent to suffer eternally, and the intimate connection of "Rufus" to the verbal command "repent" reinforces this association. In this story, as in "A Stroke of Good Fortune," "Rufus," as name, correlates with "Sufur," as well as with the sorrow, repentance, and blood-red implications implied in its biblical origins.

In addition to the play on the name of "Rufus" to code the necessity of suffering and repentance, O'Connor's language choices reinforce the continued impression of suffering paramount in the story. In this story O'Connor makes overt associations of hurt and suffering in connection with both Sheppard and Norton. The phrases, clauses, and sentences below demonstrate how O'Connor's saturates the fabric of this story with negative images of misery, despair, and anguish (my emphasis):

> "The lame'll carry off the *prey*!" . . .
>
> like a man who has been *shot* . . .
>
> he had not *spared* himself, he had *sacrificed* . . .
>
> *Foulness* hung about him . . .
>
> He was *swept* with a sudden *panic*.
>
> as if it were the voice of his *accuser*.
>
> each syllable like a *dull blow*.
>
> His mouth *twisted* . . .
>
> Norton's face rose before him, *empty*, *forlorn*, his left eye *listing* . . . as if it could not bear a full view of *grief*.
>
> His heart *constricted* with a *repulsion* for himself so clear and intense that he *gasped for breath*.
>
> His image of himself *shrivelled* . . .
>
> He sat there *paralyzed*, aghast.
>
> A rush of *agonizing* love for the child rushed over him like a *transfusion* of life.
>
> He *groaned* . . .
>
> He would never let him *suffer* again. (*CS* 481-82)

But how can we read Norton's suicide as an acceptable finale to this young boy's suffering? In Catholic theology, suicide is the ultimate sin of despair, a mortal sin. Sinners who die with mortal sins on their souls become forever damned to the eternal fires of hell deprived everlastingly of the sight of God. In fact, in O'Connor's day, the body of the sinner committing such an act was even denied burial in the consecrated ground of a Catholic cemetery. Norton cannot be forgiven for this sin. Nor is it possible to consider him an innocent child unaware of the terrible consequences of his transgression since O'Connor pointedly makes clear from the beginning of the story that Norton was a "stocky blond boy of ten," three years beyond the Catholic age of reason from which time sins can knowingly be committed. Norton, who was so terrified of hell that he begged Rufus to repent receives no mercy from O'Connor. His association with suffering on earth seems of no avail. His sin is so great he can never rejoin his mother in heaven, yet we cannot help but pity this child. Norton, like Ruby in "A Stroke of Good Fortune" seems worthy of our compassion. Surprisingly, no overt Catholic admonition against committing suicide is apparent in this O'Connor story.

O'Connor's language emphasizes the concept of "suffering" in connection with Sheppard as an indication that he must finally recognize his sins, and that suffering must become a conscious experience for him. The continuous references to behavior and conditions that would cause suffering for both Sheppard and Norton throughout this final passage in the story reinforce the premise that Rufus was sent to Sheppard as an instrument of suffering, a condition that must occur before Sheppard is able to repent. One must wonder, however, if O'Connor intends Sheppard to meet Norton's fate; she chooses to describe him as "a man on the edge of a pit" when he discovers Norton's body. Can the reader safely assume that Sheppard, who has believed heaven to be a lie throughout the story, will now step back from that pit transformed into a believer? He has just discovered his dead son, who he only recently realized needed his love and attention. The reader might expect that this father, who had not attended to either the emotional or spiritual needs of his son, might find his final suffering unendurable and instead be plunged into the depths of despair not only at the loss of his son, but at the appalling realization that his neglect caused this horrifying tragedy. Despite the fact that O'Connor makes suffering available to Sheppard, and she would see suffering as essential for forgiveness and redemption, it seems implausible that this catastrophic blow will surface as the means of rescuing Sheppard's soul.

"Rufus" emerges as anagram in both "A Stroke of Good Fortune" and "The Lame Shall Enter First" presumably serving as the embodiment of the suffering O'Connor surely intends her characters to endure before they can be cleansed of their sins and be worthy to enter the kingdom of heaven. As readers, however, we encounter disparities and confusion as we try to juggle what we assume to be O'Connor's intent with what we encounter textually. O'Connor's propensity for negation severely challenges the reader to find the holy in these fictional settings. Her love of word play and mystery would lead one to expect that the challenge is intentional and that anagram may well be one of the important fictional devices O'Connor employs to embed her meaning in complexities, but in these two stories the reader cannot infer that suffering for these characters is sufficient for their atonement.

The word "mystery" encompasses concealment, secrecy, the unknown and the unknowable, and for O'Connor this word was intimately connected to religion and spirituality. She emphasized her view of mystery in a 1959 letter to Cecil Dawkins:

> Dogma is the guardian of mystery. The doctrines are spiritually significant in ways that we cannot fathom. According to St. Thomas, prophetic vision is not a matter of seeing clearly, but of seeing what is distant, hidden. (*Collected* 1116)

O'Connor's style guards her fictional message with language implicitly intended to relate spiritual mystery with conceptual mystery, but decoding that style remains a problem for readers not privileged to know her auctorial design. These brief and partial selections from the opening of "Greenleaf" illustrate how O'Connor conceals mystery in the ordinary:

> The window was dark . . .
>
> Clouds . . . blackened him . . .
>
> in the dark . . .
>
> the moon drifted into retirement . . .
>
> There was nothing to mark his place . . .
>
> standing . . . behind the blind . . .
>
> he never appeared . . .
>
> some invisible circle . . .
>
> she had always doubted . . .

she didn't even like to think. (*CS* 311-13)

The story ends with similarly descriptive language:

> She did not understand why . . .
>
> wondering . . . why . . .
>
> she didn't think . . .
>
> probably . . .
>
> suppose . . .
>
> something emerged . . .
>
> a black heavy shadow . . .
>
> She looked beyond him to see if . . .
>
> she called and looked . . . to see if . . .
>
> unbelief . . .
>
> as if she could not decide . . .
>
> she was not looking . . .
>
> some invisible circle . . .
>
> she seemed . . .
>
> whispering some last discovery. (*CS* 332-34)

Despite the clues presented to Mrs. May throughout the story that should have told her that her life needed reevaluation, Mrs. May seems to have made little progress in uncovering the mystery that pursues her. On the final page of the story, O'Connor uses the word "tired" five times in reference to Mrs. May's state of being, yet Mrs. May "does not understand why" this is so. O'Connor's language determines the unavailability of the clues that mask from both Mrs. May and the reader an awareness of what will be her fate. Mrs. May's world, both in the beginning and the end of this story, is enveloped in a haze of secrecy. She continues to *wonder why*, to *suppose*, to be surrounded by "*some invisible* circle," and she is last seen whispering "*some* . . . discovery" into the bull's ear. Mystery becomes palpable in O'Connor's language and becomes the impediment to total understanding for Mrs. May and the readers who try to decipher the circumstances that surround her. Mystery, through language ambiguities, is the tangible aspect of Mrs. May's world even in her death. There is little reason for the reader to suppose that Mrs. May finally discovers the truth as she lies dying when she had been unable to do so while she lived.

O'Connor's grammar of negation also encompasses language choices that point toward an underlying directional bias for movement "down" as opposed to "up," an implied metaphorical structure pervasive in Western culture that builds on the idea that God/paradise is up and Satan/hell is down.[12] Additionally, the belief that "the future will be better" is a cultural value intrinsic to Western society that George Lakoff and Mark Johnson believe positively equates with the "up-down" philosophy, a concept pertinent to O'Connor's message. This consideration of the future most certainly supports the Christian idea that the future of the everlasting soul for one who has lived a life according to Christian teachings includes a life after death happily spent in heaven with the Creator.

In "A Good Man Is Hard to Find," the ending of the story alludes to a variety of "up" and "down" references, but the predominance of "down" is significant:

> 1. the grandmother raised her head . . .
>
> 2. "Jesus was the only One that ever raised the dead."
>
> 3. "enjoy the few minutes you got left the best way you can—by killing somebody or burning down his house . . ."

---

[12]See George Lakoff and Mark Johnson, *Metaphors We Live By* (Chicago: University of Chicago Press, 1980) 14-22 for a fuller discussion of the metaphoric structure of "up" and "down."

4. "Maybe He didn't raise the dead," the old lady mumbled . . . feeling so dizzy that she sank down in the ditch with her legs twisted under her.

5. hitting the ground with his fist.

6. "Listen lady," he said in a high voice. . . .

7. Then he put his gun down on the ground. . . .

8. Hiram and Bobby Lee returned from the woods and stood over the ditch, looking down at the grandmother who half sat and half lay in a puddle of blood with her legs crossed under her like a child's and her face smiling up at the cloudless sky.

9. "She was a talker, wasn't she?" Bobby Lee said, sliding down the ditch . . . (*CS* 132, for sentences 1-8; 133 for sentence 9.)

The sense of "downness" predominates in this concluding section of the story. Only four directional references indicate an "up" orientation:

sentence 1 raised her head
sentence 2 raised the dead
sentence 6 high voice
sentence 8 stood over; smiling up.

The remaining references all express a "downness":

sentence 3 burning down
sentence 4 didn't raise; sank down; ditch; under
sentence 5 ground
sentence 7 down on the ground
sentence 8 ditch; looking down; sat; lay; under
sentence 9 sliding down the ditch.

O'Connor's directional words point us "downward." Even those sentences that express a connection with "up" are tentative about the legitimacy of this motion. Sentence 2, spoken by The Misfit, and containing the directional concept of "up," seems to negate its "upness" because it is followed by the negative sentence "and He shouldn't have done it," along with a succeeding series of "ifs" that indicate his skepticism. And sentence 6, while also indicating the concept "up" in the reference to The Misfit's "high" voice presents certain problems in asserting its "upness." This sentence, too, is directly followed by the word "if," and to compound the ambiguity of O'Connor's intentions, the only other reference to The Misfit's voice in the paragraph describes it as "becom[ing] almost a snarl," an action associated with a downward turn of the lips. Moreover, sentence 8, with its two references to "up," not only predominately indicates "down" because of the grandmother's lifeless posture, but, because the word "under" appears as intimately associated with the word "crossed," perhaps subtly implies the burying of religious imagery.

For O'Connor's characters the concept of "down" infuses their world with a desperate and depressing ambience that suggests that the future is *not* better. In fact for them, there is often no future, only a dreary, miserable present. O'Connor's negative outlook pervades her linguistic structures and departs from the traditional Catholic view of future everlasting spiritual life. In most of her fiction, her characters lead lives without promise, and any hope for salvation is tangled in a grammar of negation that cloaks their fate in mystery and mires them in hopelessness. O'Connor's characters struggle with sin and folly, and if they are given a revelation of God's mystery, this moment is overcast in murky references to the unhappiness, depravity, and depression associated with the predominating linguistic structures that seem to present the concept "down" as a discernible impression of despair. In "A Good Man Is Hard to Find" Red Sammy's wife says, "It isn't a soul in this green world of God's that you can trust" (*CS* 122). This sentence typifies the dichotomy present in O'Connor's fiction. O'Connor may mean to infer that only trust in God and the hereafter will lead souls to redemption; instead, her language presents souls seemingly stalled by a grammar of negation in a world not even green, unable to free themselves and unnoticed by God.

6.
The Verbal Structure of Infinity

Christian literature has often figured eternal time as a circle in which all moments are part of an eternal now. In *Time and the Narrative* Paul Ricoeur recounts that "Augustine celebrates the eternity of the Word that remains when our words pass away."[1] Ricoeur notes also that Aristotle's "assertion that the instant determines time is said to have begun the series of definitions of time as a sequence of 'nows,' in the sense of indistinguishable instants."[2] Time can also be perceived as having linear progression. As John F. Desmond explains:

> [The] biblical view [of] history is evolutionary: it has a beginning, a specific point of transforming apotheosis (the Incarnation), and a definite end (the Last Judgment). History's direction is therefore linear. Such a view subsumes the cyclical notions of history . . .[3]

Desmond's depiction of an evolutionary biblical view is relevant to the historical view of the various Christian religions that advocate moving toward the final judgment, a conceptual premise easily accessible to the finite human mind. However, the linearity of historical direction does not preclude that in religious terms, eternal time has neither forward nor backward movement but only an ever present now. Northrop Frye indicates that

> Jesus' teaching recurs often to the fact that human life, whether cyclical in shape or not, is a confused and inseparable mixture of joy and suffering, good and evil, life and death, and that the eternal realities of this life are its two poles, worlds of life and death which are outside time.[4]

Eternal time, therefore, in relation to God, the alpha and omega, considered by Christian religions as encompassing all of infinity, can be

---

[1]Paul Ricoeur, *Time and Narrative*, 3 vols. (Chicago: University of Chicago Press, 1985) 3:264.

[2]Ibid., 88.

[3]Desmond, *Risen Sons*, 8.

[4]Northrop Frye, *The Great Code: The Bible and Literature* (New York: Harcourt Brace Jovanovich, Publishers, 1982) 72.

measured in spiritual terms as being outside of historical time and represented diagrammatically as the perfect circle rather than the line straining to reach an endpoint. In a 1956 letter to "A," O'Connor writes:

> I have been reading about eternity in a book of Jean Guitton's called The Virgin Mary . . . and have had considerable light thrown on the subject for me. He says that eternity begins in time and that we must stop thinking of it as something that follows time. (*Collected* 1001)

O'Connor's literary works deal rather surreptitiously with time in both narrative observances and eternal suggestions and can be analyzed in respect to their linear or circular patterns.

O'Connor's verbal structures parallel the time references inherent in her fictional representations. Through her verb choices, verb forms, and tense decisions, she masterfully suggests the enfolding of linear human time into the circle of eternal time. Yet while O'Connor's fiction depicting lives bound to the world is necessarily secured to a narrative linear development of plot structure and sequential time, the ultimate outgrowth of her grammatical choices intimates the circle of God and the timelessness of the moment of Grace. The artistic problem she so skillfully circumvents is how to show as verbal form in her fiction, the circle of God's eternity within the line of finite human history.

Desmond feels that "O'Connor struggled with, in, and toward this biblical vision throughout the process of making her fiction."[5] And May suggests that O'Connor relied on the biblical parable to transmit her message. He observes that

> The word-orientation of O'Connor's fiction, moreover, is basically scriptural in inspiration and parabolic in effect. The specific New Testament literary form that her art imitates is the parable, where religious meaning is structured in terms of human conflict symbolizing man's relationship with God. For what the parables of Jesus reveal to the listener is that life is gained or lost in the midst of everyday existence.[6]

---

[5]Desmond, *Risen Sons*, 12.

[6]May, *The Pruning Word*, xxiv.

If we can assume that O'Connor wished to convey a biblical view of history, which by Desmond's definition has an evolutionary design, her actual narrative structure becomes problematic to the reader. While O'Connor may have intended to pattern the structure of her fiction after her historical biblical view, and her fictional message is, indeed, often presented as parable, her vision as gleaned from her fictional structure was, in fact, circular. The concept of linearity in human time is inextricably bound to the movement of plot in O'Connor's fiction, and this temporal arrangement as contained in her narrative structure conflicts with her circular view of eternity.

Structural features of O'Connor's fiction require a progressive narrative as her characters move toward their redemptive reunion with God. Her narrative structure is bound by beginnings, development, and conclusions, but her fictional characters bypass a linear progression toward heaven and their Creator to find a timeless moment in which line encloses itself to form the circle of eternity. The action of grace and the moment in which grace is extended is apocalyptic and, hence, atemporal, and the question facing the reader is whether O'Connor's characters find themselves included or excluded from God's circular embrace.

One of the most apparent examples of how O'Connor tries to solve the problem of finding a circular fictional structure occurs in the novel *Wise Blood*. In the opening scene of this novel, Hazel Motes is alone on a train with Mrs. Wally Bee Hitchcock, an older woman, who surmises that Haze is "going home" (*Collected* 3). In her desire to learn more about him, "she found herself squinting . . . at his eyes, trying almost to look into them" (*Collected* 3). O'Connor's narration continues with statements that emphasize the description of Haze's eyes and his person:

> They were the color of pecan shells and set in deep sockets. The outline of a skull under his skin was plain and insistent. (*Collected* 3)

The focus of Mrs. Hitchcock's interest remains in Haze's eyes which

> held her attention longest. Their settings were so deep that they seemed, to her, almost like passages leading somewhere and she leaned halfway across the space that separated the two seats, trying to see into them. (*Collected* 4)

O'Connor concludes this story with a scene that duplicates the opening one, ending Haze's fictional existence as it began. Haze, now dead, is alone with a woman, Mrs. Flood, his landlady, who discusses his homecoming. She says to him, "Well, Mr. Motes, . . . I see you've come home!" (*Collected* 131). Mrs. Flood, like Mrs. Hitchcock, is fascinated by Haze's eyes and "leaned closer and closer to his face looking deep into them, trying to see how she had been cheated or what had cheated her, but she couldn't see anything" (*Collected* 131). And once again O'Connor echoes the statement used in the opening episode with a reference to the long passageway of which Mrs. Hitchcock had also become aware: "The outline of a skull was plain under his skin and the deep burned eye sockets seemed to lead into the dark tunnel where he had disappeared" (*Collected* 131).

The circular structure of O'Connor's fiction is apparent not only in *Wise Blood* but also in many of her short stories. The opening episode of "A Stroke of Good Fortune" presents Ruby, in a state of exhaustion, poised at the bottom of the stairwell, unable to move. She disgustingly utters, "'Collard greens!'. . . spitting the word from her mouth this time as if it were a poisonous seed" (*Collected* 184). The collard greens are a connection to her brother, Rufus, and he, as her baby brother, is a connection to her hate and fear of children. The implication of the words "spitting . . . from her mouth . . . a poisonous seed" reflects her disdaining attitude toward the seed of life she carries within her, which will become evident later on in the story. But the Word, which is God, is also the "seed" that Ruby expectorates in her intentional flaunting of the Catholic rule against the use of birth control.

The ending of this story reproduces the opening details, a duplication perhaps intended to reinforce the reproductive cycle in which Ruby is now engaged. The circular circumstances surrounding Ruby become conspicuous. As the story ends, Ruby is again too exhausted to negotiate the stairs. She has made it to the top, but her focus remains "down to the very bottom where she had started up so very long ago" (*Collected* 196). Her utterance of the word "'Baby'" is connected to the word "leered" and accompanied with the cavernous images of hollowness and despair and with statements previously associated with Rufus's destruction of her mother. Her rejection echoes her view of the child she carries as a "poisonous seed," and once more encircles a word, reminiscent of T. S. Eliot's phrase in "Gerontion" of "The word within a word, unable to speak a word,/Swaddled with darkness." Therefore, while Ruby has technically reached the top of the stairs, structurally the implication is that she remains "where she started up so very long ago." Her upward movement only circles her back to her beginnings. She makes no progress toward the evolutionary goal that Desmond describes, but neither does the circularity of the story complete the image of God's wholeness. Ruby's circles are not true circles in a theological sense as they become, instead, a vortex pulling her down to an ever-narrowing point of annihilation.

The story "Greenleaf" also creates circular impressions. The opening scene begins with the bull likened to a "patient god" clouded in darkness with a "lowered . . . head," pawing the ground (*CS* 311). His final description duplicates his initial one as the charging bull "emerged from the tree line, a black heavy shadow" with "his head lowered" intent on his mission to infuse Mrs. May with divine light (*CS* 333). Other images reinforce the circular movement of the action in this story. The "invisible circle" first drawn in connection with Mr. Greenleaf at the beginning of the story, completes its circumference at the end. Mr. Greenleaf

> walked with a high-shouldered creep and he never appeared to come directly forward. He walked on the perimeter of some invisible circle . . . (*CS* 313)

As Mrs. May lies dying, gored by the bull, the same invisible circle appears again in connection with Mr. Greenleaf:

> Mr. Greenleaf was running toward her from the side with his gun raised and she saw him coming though she was not looking in his direction. She saw him approaching on the outside of some invisible circle, the tree line gaping behind him and nothing under his feet. (*CS* 334)

Episodically, Mrs. May seems not to have entered the circle in which she would dwell with God. The movement of the story parallels her movement along a line toward damnation instead of into the circle of the heavenly bull.

"A View of the Woods" presents similar circular patterns. The narration begins with the information that Mary Fortune and Mr. Fortune "spent every morning watching the machine that lifted out dirt and threw it in a pile" (*CS* 335). O'Connor describes the scene surrounding this occurrence:

> The red corrugated lake eased up to within fifty feet of the construction and was bordered on the other side by a black line of woods which appeared at both ends of the view to walk across the water and continue along the edge of the fields. (*CS* 335)

The construction machinery holds a fascination for Mary Fortune who was

> watching the big disembodied gullet gorge itself on the clay, then, with the sound of a deep sustained nausea and a slow mechanical revulsion, turn and spit it up. (*CS* 335)

These images are repeated as the story comes to its conclusion. Mr. Fortune "saw that the gaunt trees had thickened into mysterious dark files that were marching across the water and away into the distance" (*CS* 356). He finally comes to realize that while an opening appears to allow him access to the lake, "he could not swim and that he had not bought the boat" (*CS* 356). As Mr. Fortune tries to summon help before he dies, he finds himself alone "except for one huge yellow monster which sat to the side, as stationary as he was, gorging itself on clay" (*CS* 356). The images available to Mr. Fortune at the beginning of the story do not provide him with insights to make changes in his life. He dies as he has lived, surrounded by the same imagery, completing the circle of inactivity, consumed by his sins.

Sentence structure in O'Connor's fiction serves to complement O'Connor's circular design. As discussed in chapter 1, the most common sentence structure used by O'Connor is a simple sentence that has "only one full predication in the form of an independent clause."[7] Compound sentences with "two or more full predications in the form of independent clauses" are also widespread in her fiction.[8] But for O'Connor, a predication most often uses an intransitive verb, which "does not require an object" and, consequently, has no receiver of the verbal action or achieves the completion of a goal.[9] The definitions of transitive and intransitive verbs are pertinent to an understanding of what is structurally significant in O'Connor's fiction. Marilyn N. Silva defines transitive verbs as:

---

[7]Frank, *Modern English*, 223.
[8]Ibid.
[9]Ibid., 49.

> verbs that are followed by at least one free NP (that is, an NP [noun phrase] not already bound to a preposition within a prepositional phrase). Semantically speaking, this free NP indicates a sentence participant directly affected by the action expressed in the verb itself.[10]

In contrast, Silva indicates that

> *Intransitive verbs* are not followed by free NPs in the predicate phrase. A sentence whose verb is intransitive indicates that a subject NP is doing something that directly affects only itself . . .[11]

While the use of an object (or as Silva terms it, a free NP in the predicate phrase) is not obligatory in English sentence structure, and intransitive verbs are not uncommon, O'Connor's sentence structure seems unusually weighted on the side of intransitivity. O'Connor also employs a large number of coordinating conjunctions which connect simple verbs in her simple sentences and independent clauses in her compound sentences.

Marcella Frank defines a sentence as:

> *a full predication containing a subject plus a predicate with a finite verb.* Its arrangement may be symbolized by such formulas as S V O (subject + verb + object), N_1 V N_2 (noun + verb + noun), or NP + VP (noun phrase + verb phrase).[12]

Using Frank's first formula as a guide, O'Connor's simple sentence structures can often be diagrammed as S + V + (and) + V, and her compound sentences as S + V + [O](and) + S + V. The sentence "Mr. Greenleaf paused with the wheelbarrow and looked behind him" illustrates the first sentence pattern of one subject (Mr. Greenleaf) with two verbs (paused, looked) connected by the conjunction "and" (*CS* 322). The sentence "The sour odor reached him and he drew back" illustrates the second sentence pattern of two complete independent clauses, each with subject and verb (where one of the independent clauses sometimes has an optional object) connected by the conjunction "and" (*CS* 449).

---

[10]Marilyn N. Silva, *Grammar in Many Voices* (Lincolnwood IL: NTC Publishing Group, 1995) 31.

[11]Ibid., 32.

[12]Frank, *Modern English*, 220.

In "Everything That Rises Must Converge," a story title that denounces linearity, O'Connor's sentence structure, upon examination, relinquishes a circular interpretation that has been deeply embedded in the structural design. In the ending to this story, O'Connor's sentence constructions overwhelmingly employ verbs that express intransitivity, forcing the focus back to the subject completing the character's circular movement rather than a linear one. When Julian realizes that his mother is experiencing a serious medical problem, O'Connor structures the following sentences on the last page of the story to incorporate mainly intransitive verb forms in his responses to her condition:

1. He looked into her face and caught his breath.

2. He was looking into a face he had never seen before.

3. He stared, stricken.

4. Stunned, he let her go . . .

5. "Mother!" he cried.

6. "Darling, sweetheart, wait!"

7. He dashed forward and fell at her side, crying, "Mamma, Mamma!"

8. He turned her over.

9. "Wait here, wait here!" he cried and jumped up and began to run for help toward a cluster of lights he saw in the distance ahead of him.

10. "Help, help!" he shouted, but his voice was thin . . .

11. he ran and his feet moved numbly as if they carried him nowhere. (*CS* 420)

These sentences or partial sentences are divided into subject, verb, and object (or expressed goal) as follows:

SUBJECT		VERB	OBJECT
1. He		looked	her face
	and	caught	his breath
2. He		was looking	–
he		had never seen	–
3. He		stared	–
4. he		let	her
5. he		cried	–
6. Darling, sweetheart		wait	–
7. He		dashed	–
	and	fell	
8. He		turned	her
9. [you]		wait	–
[you]		wait	–
he		cried	–
	and	jumped up	–
	and	began to run	–
he		saw	–
10. [you]		Help	–
[you]		help	–
he		shouted	–
[his] voice		was	–
11. he		ran	–
[his] feet		moved	–
they		carried	him.

Twenty-one (84%) of the twenty-five verbs used in this section are intransitive and, therefore, require no direct object (or free NP) to complete the verbal actions. Semantically the intransitive verb cannot transfer the action initiated by the subject to an object, which thrusts the unrealized verbal action back onto the subject—creating not a linear progression, but a circular pattern. Of the four verbs that are transitive, only sentence 8 (He turned her over.) indicates a conscious, deliberate, overt linear action on Julian's part. The transitive verb in the first sentence (He . . . caught his breath.) describes an involuntary action beyond Julian's control and one which captures that which he already possessed —his own breath. Sentence 4 (he let her go), while syntactically indicating an object of the verb, or a goal achieved by Julian as the subject or doer of this action, nonetheless, semantically indicates an action actually performed by

Julian's mother. And sentence 11, the final use of a transitive verb in connection with Julian, is an action preformed by Julian's feet, and structurally becomes reflexive.

Critics have varied opinions about Julian's "moment of grace." Feeley states that this "story shows the 'rising' of Julian's mother, and, by implication, his own."[13] May agrees that Julian will acknowledge his transgressions and, after a time, find God. He writes:

> As his mother crumples to the pavement, the horror of his sin breaks upon him like the ominous dawn of a dark day of grief. Julian, in panic, runs down the street for help, but the tide of darkness "seems to sweep him back to her, postponing from moment to moment his entry into the world of guilt and sorrow." We are led to believe that Julian will, indeed, enter that world. Nevertheless, the extent of his sin, measured by the horrifying judgment leveled against him, must necessarily prolong his period of purgation.[14]

While Feeley sees Julian's redemption more tenuously than May does, as indicated by her use of the words "by implication" to refer to his spiritual fate, both consider that Julian, after a stint in Purgatory, will eventually achieve salvation. Kessler, however, puts Julian into an even more tenuous state for he indicates that at the end of this story, "Julian becomes inarticulate and directionless. . . . [and] caught between two states of consciousness, [he] must wait—even for his suffering."[15] Desmond feels more strongly that Julian's "last move is the reverse of the movement into history we see in Haze Motes and in young Tarwater."[16] And Gentry believes that Julian's "redemption, if it occurs, must come from outside."[17]

If O'Connor's purpose is to imply Julian's movement toward eventual salvation, her verb forms contradict this intent. Intransitive verbs inhibit Julian from achieving earthly goals and from making any spiritual progress. In the final episode of this story, Julian is intimately associated with self-contained intransitivity. The structural composition of sentences that lack recipiency of the verbal actions obligated by the absence of

---

[13]Feeley, *Voice of the Peacock*, 105.

[14]May, *The Pruning Word*, 96-97.

[15]Kessler, *Flannery O'Connor and the Language of the Apocalypse,* 124-25.

[16]Desmond, *Risen Sons*, 71.

[17]Gentry, *Flannery O'Connor's Religion of the Grotesque*, 99.

direct objects insinuates a spiritual condition that parallels Julian's earthly one. He is unable to move forward toward his salvation. O'Connor's intransitivity imparts subtle, almost imperceptible linguistic overtones of doubt upon the actuality of Julian's redemption by refocusing on Julian as an actor without accomplishments. The intransitive verbs only act "to sweep [Julian] back" to the moment of his sinful beginnings, reflecting the state of his immortal soul. If the death of his mother is intended to signify that Julian has moved outside linear time and beyond his sins, the verbs expose the falsity of evolutionary time and stop movement in the still circle. Julian makes no spiritual progress. He ends the story where he began, securely tethered within his circle of sin. The problem for readers and critics alike is to decide what prevails here: the narrative and thematic evolution, or the circularity of God's design. The title of the story, in which all apparent lines converge, may be the accepted guide as to how to read O'Connor's intent, but the abundance of intransitive verbs gives pause to this rendering.

O'Connor's fiction is ladened with intransitive verbs. In "Good Country People" from the moment Hulga realizes that Manley Pointer may not be "just good country people" until his disappearance across the lake, eighty-four main verbs are used; of these verbs, forty-six are intransitive (55%). Although this figure is considerably lower than the number of intransitive verbs used in the ending of "Everything That Rises Must Converge," the majority of the thirty-eight verbs used transitively (twenty-six or 68%) refer to actions completed by the Bible salesman. These transitive verbs with their accompanying direct objects semantically propel the Bible salesman in a linear fashion toward his eternal destiny. As a measure of how shut out of the kingdom of heaven he is, it is the Bible salesman who:

> sell[s] Bibles . . . sweep[s] the cards . . . throw[s] the Bible . . . grab[s] the leg . . . slammed the lid and snatched up the valise and swung it . . . regarded her . . . got a woman's glass eye . . . use[d] a different name . . . and [has] been believing in nothing. (*CS* 290-91)

In contrast to the active will the Bible salesman exercises to sink himself in the linear world of temporality, the verbs surrounding Hulga suggest that her fate is beyond her volition, and that she is subject to God. Of the transitive verbs used in connection with Hulga, most of the completed actions refer to situations beyond her control or are neutralized by their semantic implications. In the sentence "Her voice when she spoke had an almost pleading sound," "voice" is the subject of the verb "had," and the word "sound" is the object completing the verbal action (*CS* 290). However, the verb "had" semantically indicates possession and thus acts as a linking verb connecting "voice" with "sound." Hulga, through grammatical structure, is forced into a circular pattern. The remainder of the sentence contains an intransitive verb in the adverbial clause "when she spoke" and reinforces the nebulous time reference that directs Hulga's progress. The construction of this intransitive clause prohibits the subject "she," Hulga as an individual, from realizing any attainments of her own, placing her in the control of another.

Other sentence constructions in this passage do contain transitive uses of the verb in connection with Hulga. These sentences with transitive verbs are:

1. she might be trying to insult him.

2. [you] say one thing and do another.

3. "Give me my leg!" [repeated 3 times]

4. she barely saw him . . .

5. She saw him grab the leg and then she saw it . . .

6. When she turned her churning face . . ., she saw his blue figure. . . (*CS* 290-91)

However, while the use of transitive verbs should provide Hulga with an opportunity to achieve her own goals and, therefore, maintain control of her own fate, this is not the case. The use of "might" in sentence 1 mitigates the verbal intent by suggesting only a possibility, not a certainty. Sentence 2, uttered by Hulga, refers to actions that can only be completed by the Bible salesman or his kind. In the imperative sentence 3, Hulga makes a demand of the Bible salesman for an object (leg) he now controls and does not intend to release. "Leg," is thus invalidated as the realization of the verbal action, perhaps a subtle reminder that what Hulga is in danger of losing is her soul and not her leg. And the adverbial clause of sentence 6 indicates a reflexive action since "she" and "face" both refer to Hulga, and are intrinsically one. All remaining sentences, (sentences 4, 5, and the main clause of 6) do allow the pronoun "she" to complete the action of the verb "saw"; however, this verb of perception only indicates a mental awareness on the part of the actor. No overt action, in the true sense of the word, is indicated with the verb "saw," though the verb, at the same time, implies the presence of what has been revealed. Therefore, despite the structurally transitive sentences that express "action" in connection with Hulga, she remains statically returned as subject by a will outside her own that implicitly sets up the action. Hulga has been forced into impotency within the circle while Manley Pointer continues along his linear path to hell.

In addition to sentences that contain intransitive verbs as a means of expressing the stillness of the eternal moment, O'Connor also uses coordinating conjunctions to design verb phrases that move the designated actor in a circle of action that encloses all. In "A Circle in the Fire," O'Connor's style reflects her message. When Mrs. Cope first becomes aware of the devastation Powell and his vandalous friends have inflicted upon her property, O'Connor's sentence structure persistently employs the coordinating conjunction "and" to create compound verbs and compound sentence constructions. Beginning with the last paragraph on page 192 of *The Complete Stories*, this final section uses twenty sentences until the end of the story. Within these sentences O'Connor uses the coordinating conjunction "and" twenty-one times. If we look at an outline of just the subjects, verbs, verbals, objects, and clauses connected by "and" in the thirteen out of the twenty sentences in this section where "and" occurs, the following pattern develops:

S+V+[O]+	Coord. Conj. + [S]	+V+[O]
1. they stopped	and	collected the matches
	and	began to set the brush . . .
2. They began to whoop	and	holler
	and	beat their hands
	and there	was a narrow line
		between her
	and	them.
3. it reached up . . .		
snatching	and	
biting . . .		

4. The wind carried the rags	and the boys	
		disappeared . . .
5. She turned	and	tried to run
	and she	stood . . .
7. Mrs. Cope	and	
Mrs. Pritchard were . . .		
8. She shrieked	and Mrs. Pritchard pointed . . .	
10. Mr. Pritchard came out	and the Negroes	stopped filling the manure spreader
	and	started . . .
13. They passed her	and	headed off . . .
16. Culver said	and they	thrust their shoulders
	and	went . . .
17. The child came	and	stared . . .
18. it looked	and it	looked . . .
19. The child turned	and she	could see the column rising
	and	widening . . .
20. She stood	and	could catch a few . . . shrieks . . .

If we consider the sentence constructions used after the coordinating conjunction "and," we find that ten of the twenty-two conjunctions (45%) are followed by verbs without a directly expressed subject preceding them. If we add to this total the two expressed subjects that refer to nebulous subjects represented by the use of expletives (sentence 2, "there"; sentence 18, "it"), the number of verbs with no overt actor jumps to thirteen and the percentage to 59%. O'Connor's use of the coordinating conjunction "and" magnifies the intransitivity of her verbal structures. The subject of each succeeding verb must return full circle to the beginning of the sentence in search of an actor to perform all ensuing actions. If this sentence structure was a conscious choice on O'Connor's part, the use of compound verbs and compound sentences masterfully emphasizes her fictional control and her ability to structure her language to echo her belief in the circularity of time and in the encompassing nature of God and eternity.

In addition to the use of intransitive verbs and coordinating conjunctions to indicate an insistence on eternal time, O'Connor employs various time references through the use of adverbials and tense selections that reinforce a perception of endless time. The ending of "The Displaced Person" contains many time references that appear to work at odds with one another. In the final section of this story, the sentence "Mrs. McIntyre was looking fixedly at Mr. Guizac's legs lying flat on the ground now" can be considered as the beginning of Mrs. McIntyre's participation into Mr. Guizac's death and, therefore, for purposes of explanation as sentence 1 of this episode (*CS* 234). What is striking about this passage is that the pastness of what has happened to Mr. Guizac, and by her inactivity what has happened to Mrs. McIntyre, is even further emphasized by the use of the past perfect tense. The past perfect is the tense used "to indicate time that precedes a particular point in a past narrative," thereby doubly stating "pastness" and implying an omniscient point of view that encloses multiple levels of time within its vision.[18] And as an additionally prominent feature, this passage contains a large number of infinitives, or the simple form of the verb (the infinitive without the "to"), both timeless verb forms which imply a "future reference with respect to the main verb" (*CS* 330).

In the twenty-one sentences of this section until the end of the story, O'Connor employs these two verb forms in twenty-eight instances (the past perfect tense ten times, the infinitive and/or simple form of the verb eighteen times). Semantically, there seems to be a conflict between these two verb usages that represent "what once was" and "what will be." To cloud the issue of time in relation to Mrs. McIntyre further, O'Connor twice includes the word "now," an indication of the present moment. Thus, the story juxtaposes past and present in narrative but absorbs them into one in the verbal structure superseding a finite human understanding

---

[18]Frank, *Modern English*, 83.

of time as past, present, and future to encompass the "eternal now" into which all time is enclosed.

Initially, the past perfect figures prominently in the concluding section of this story. This tense choice is coupled with the additional time markers and adverbial usages that exemplify O'Connor's verbal strategy. Toward the end of the story, however, the infinitive or simple form dominates. The listing of the two noticeable verb forms in this final episode appears below in their corresponding sentences (numbering begins with the last twenty-one sentences of the story (*CS* 234-35):

SENTENCE	PAST PERFECT	INFINITIVE/SIMPLE VERB
3.	had seen the Negro	jump
	had released	
	had seen Mr. Shortley	turn and stare
	had started	to shout
	had not (shouted)	
4.	had felt her eyes	come
	had heard	
5.		to help
6.	had fainted	
7.	had arrived	
9.	had come	
11.		to be
14.		to look for, to see
16.		to go
17.		to run, to live, to save
18.		to jiggle, to stay, to wait on
20.		to come out, to see.
21.	had fed	

It is significant that the future commitment implied by the infinitive or simple form of the verb appears concentrated in the last part of the story while the past perfect, at this point, has all but disappeared into an implied constant present. And since O'Connor saves the meting out of justice and the offering of grace until the end of her stories, this use of the infinitive in the latter part of this story seems to connect Mrs. McIntyre's future spiritual destiny with the infinite moment.

However, O'Connor still continues an insistence on the past with the use of the verb "remember" which is used four times in the entire passage. One of these appearances occurs in the penultimate sentence:

> Not many people remembered to come out to the country to see her except the old priest. (*CS* 235)

To connect "remember," a verb that emphasizes the past, with two infinitives that should emphasize the future, seems to bring the action of the future as contained in the infinitives back into the past completing a circular motion which contains both past and future. Other instances of "pastness" occur with the infinitives in this final passage. Sentence 14 reads as follows:

> That evening, Mr. Shortley left without notice to look for a new position and the Negro, Sulk, was taken with a sudden desire to see more of the world and set off for the southern part of the state. (*CS* 235)

To indicate a specific time in the past, as does the phrase "That evening," requires an anchoring of the action to the past. And sentence 17 acts in a like manner:

> When she came back, she saw that the place would be too much for her to run now and she turned her cows over to a professional auctioneer (who sold them at a loss) and retired to live on what she had, while she tried to save her declining health. (*CS* 235)

The time markers, "When she came back," and "while" both affix a past reading on the three infinitives in this sentence. "When" indicates a dependency upon the action with which it is coupled. In this passage, the action occurred in the past; therefore, creating a linkage to the past before the ensuing action (also in the past) can be effected. The adverb, "while," also present in this same sentence, carries with it the meaning of continuing at the same time, and because of the initial focus of "when" in the beginning of the sentence, it, too, conveys past implications. Sentence 18 also accentuates the past:

> A numbness developed in one of her legs and her hands and head began to jiggle and eventually she had to stay in bed all the time with only a colored woman to wait on her. (*CS* 235)

Both "eventually" and "all the time" denote a finality associated with a past happening. And sentence 19 continues with this emphasis of the past moving to overtake the future:

> Her eyesight grew steadily worse and she lost her voice all together. (*CS* 235)

The final sentence, sentence 21, seems to bring Mrs. McIntyre's life to its earthly completion. The action then focuses on the priest who initiates all meaningful actions in verbs and overt past references that suggest their on-going pattern:

> He came regularly once a week with a bag of breadcrumbs and, after he had fed these to the peacock, he would come in and sit by the side of her bed and explain the doctrines of the Church. (*CS* 235)

Not only is the word "after" used, which indicates "back in time," but the priest's actions expressed in past tense, past perfect, and conditional past tense are meant to be seen as repetitious. He came "regularly." He came "once a week." He "would come . . . and sit . . . and explain."

The time references and conditional past clarify O'Connor's concept of past as escaping its finite limitations and its structural confines to become conceptually continuous. The sentence structure of "The Displaced Person" mirrors O'Connor's theological view by turning the future back upon itself and thus creates an overwhelming sense of merger with the past. Such stylistic features suggest a return to one's beginnings with all human time finally forming a continuum that remains forever within the invisible circle of eternity. Though her stories move through the linear development of plot, O'Connor's style both episodically and syntactically lends credence to her belief in an eternal circle of time rather than an evolutionary historical view. She successfully harmonizes form and function by deftly integrating the concept of eternal time in its circularity within the confines of narrative linearity. Do O'Connor's characters move into the eternal circle she would wish for them or are they excluded from participation in the circumference of God's grace, remaining instead in the circle of their own sinfully created worlds and allowed only a view of the woods? The challenge facing O'Connor's readers becomes one of uncovering the mystery of whether these circles embrace everlasting salvation or the eternal flames of hell.

Conclusion

Flannery O'Connor's ability as a storyteller has long secured her a devoted following. Her intense characterizations and her talent for sustaining suspense make her a captivating writer and are among her strengths as an artist. O'Connor's critics, however, have often held varied opinions as to the impact of her fictional message. Her concern for educating and reforming an audience fallen away from religious mystery was a preoccupation that obsessively pervades her fiction. And in some ways, this passion for religion detracts from her artistic strength. For many she seems to restate continually the same message through recurring themes and plot similarities. Like any author, O'Connor displays shortcomings. Yet a linguistic analysis of her fiction reveals her immense talent as an artisan of words. Her incredible facility with the language and her considerable linguistic control of her fictional product often allow her to manipulate her fiction to accommodate her religious dogma, but her inherent integrity as an artist just as often opens possibilities of meaning that refuse the confines of her ideology. This work is an attempt to explain the paradox contained within O'Connor's fiction.

O'Connor remains an enigmatic and complex artist. Stylistically through sentence structure, parts of speech, and verb usage, O'Connor determines the salvation of her fictional characters. However, her language choices often appear to place her characters in direct opposition with her frequently expressed religious intent. An examination of the language that O'Connor chooses suggests that the conflict may very well be intentional to foster her concept of the Divine Mystery and to replicate this mystery within her fictional works. The puzzle O'Connor presents to her reading public revolves around the ostensibly inconsistent treatment her language and tropes appear to thrust upon the helpless souls within her fictional world. Her characters, through her language choices, become ensnared in a tangle of mystery on their journeys toward salvation. O'Connor's grammatical dependence on pronouns and her naming techniques often seem to assign her characters to states of invisibility. Her reliance on the verb "to be," and modals such as "might," "would," "could," and "should" either leave her characters in a state of inactivity or in a posture fraught with uncertainty. The addition of passive voice and passive intent as contained in her adjective choices again furthers the perception that her fictional characters are unable to determine their spiritual fates despite what she has stated is her commitment to free will.

Through an intimate connection with grammatical negation, passivity, and intransitivity, O'Connor manages to permeate the souls of her characters with redemptive inertia. They seem unable to accept or reject their moments of grace or share in any heavenly rewards due to the linguistic determinations imposed upon them.

The symbols and symbolic inconsistencies surrounding O'Connor's characters also often hobble them with impediments that cause readers to question their opportunities for eternal life. O'Connor's images similarly fail to provide insights into what spiritual vision is possible, or even can be possible for her characters. In O'Connor's fiction, images of violence surround those characters she considered saved as well as those characters she considered damned. Thus, readers are often required to speculate about O'Connor's message and are persistently diverted from a Catholic vision. Additionally, O'Connor's treatment of religious themes acts as a complement to her grammatical and figurative choices often refusing insight into the Catholic worldview she so fervently defended in her correspondences and lectures. She seemed consciously to employ a profound sense of mystery in a concerted attempt to embed her religious message deeply within the story creating characters whose destinies remain spiritually debatable but thus available to readers she believed religiously hostile.

In clarifying the relationship of the Old Testament to the New, Northrop Frye cites the traditional adage that in the Old Testament the New Testament is concealed; in the New, the Old revealed.[1] Flannery O'Connor's fiction miraculously duplicates this feat. Her fiction is more available to the Old Testament than to the religious values of the New, a fact which often moves her away from the doctrines accessible to modern-day Catholics. Yet this merger of old law with new was what she intentionally set out to accomplish. By manipulating verb tenses and achieving a circularity in her fictional structure, she addresses the concept of eternity through the transcendence of time, a transcendency which endeavors to move her characters into the eternal now, a state she believed we should all strive to attain.

Too often critics approach O'Connor's work as reflective of a strictly orthodox Catholic viewpoint, or with their own set agenda into which they structure her work. She herself, in her private correspondence and

---

[1]Frye, *The Great Code*, 79.

lectures, has tutored her readers to look for Catholic meanings in her work, often to the exclusion of other messages. Yet O'Connor remained committed to the development of mystery as the hallmark of a proficient writer. As she indicated in *Mystery and Manners*:

> A story is good when you continue to see more and more in it, and when it continues to escape you. In fiction two and two is always more than four. (*MM* 102)

She further quantifies a good story as one that "successfully resists paraphrase," one that "hangs on and expands in the mind" (*MM* 108). O'Connor's linguistic competence is the aspect of her fiction that enables her work to surpass this mathematical analogy exponentially. As Frederick Crews asserts:

> [W]e need to recall that [O'Connor's] first loyalty as a writer of fiction was to the cause of vivid, resonant, radically economical art. It is a measure of her success that we are still grasping at formulas that might explain, or even explain away, her electrifying power.[2]

O'Connor's talents as an artist reside in her ability to create a mystifying quality in all aspects of her fiction. She mastered the technique of cryptically presenting her religious representations as a microcosmic backdrop to the universal mystery contained in Christian dogma. The mystery that she is able to invoke magnifies the importance of her work and lends respectability to her status. As an artist, her style dislodges her from the realm of provincialism and places her within the wider literary world. If we, as critical readers, are able to step back from her counsel to acquaint ourselves with the written word on the page, O'Connor emerges as a tremendously complex writer despite her concerted attempts to appear simple and available to her reading public. O'Connor wrote to Cecil Dawkins on 23 December 1959 that "Dogma is the guardian of mystery" and to Ben Griffin on 9 July 1955 that she "relish[ed] the idea of being read by scholars" (*HB* 365; 89). These two statements assume significance as we linguistically investigate O'Connor's works. O'Connor saw herself as the guardian of Catholic dogma which she believed must

---

[2]Crews, "The Power of Flannery O'Connor," 55.

necessarily be disguised in mystery if it were to overtake the souls of her readers. The facility by which she surreptitiously wove dogmatic mystery into her fictional fabric through carefully chosen linguistic and grammatical choices ensures that scholars, overtaken by her linguistic talents, will long relish the idea of reading and discussing the mystery that is O'Connor.

Works Cited

Asals, Frederick. *Flannery O'Connor: The Imagination of Extremity.* Athens: University of Georgia Press, 1982.

Bergman, David and Daniel Mark Epstein. *The Heath Guide to Literature.* Lexington MA: D. C. Heath and Company, 1984.

Bowen, Robert O. "Hope vs. Despair in the New Gothic Novel." *Renascence: A Critical Journal of Letters* 13/3 (Spring 1961): 147-52.

Boyd, Zelda, "The Grammar of Representation in Psychoanalysis and Literature." In *The Psychoanalytic Study of Literature*, edited by Joseph Reppen and Maurice Charney, 107-124. Hillsdale NJ: Analytic Press, 1985.

Brooks, Peter. "The Idea of a Psychoanalytic Literary Criticism." In *Discourse in Psychoanalysis and Literature*, edited by Shlomith Rimmon-Kenan, 1-8. London: Methuen & Co. Ltd., 1987.

Cluett, Robert. *Prose Style and Critical Reading.* New York: Teachers College Press, 1976.

Crews, Frederick. "The Power of Flannery O'Connor." *The New York Review of Books* 37/7 (26 April 1990): 49-55.

Cugno, Alain. *Saint John of the Cross: The Life and Thought of a Christian Mystic.* London: Burns & Oates, 1979.

Deedy, John. *The Catholic Fact Book.* Chicago: Thomas More Press, 1986.

Desmond, John F. *Risen Sons: Flannery O'Connor's Vision of History.* Athens: University of Georgia Press, 1987.

Dillon, George L. *Language Processing and the Reading of Literature: Toward a Model of Comprehension.* Bloomington: Indiana University Press, 1978.

Dolan, Jay P. *The American Catholic Experience: A History from Colonial Times to the Present.* New York: Doubleday & Company, Inc., 1985.

Eggenschwiler, David. *The Christian Humanism of Flannery O'Connor.* Detroit: Wayne State University Press, 1972.

Fawcett, Thomas. *The Symbolic Language of Religion: An Introductory Study.* London: SCM Press Ltd., 1970.

Feeley, Kathleen. *Flannery O'Connor: Voice of the Peacock.* New Brunswick: Rutgers University Press, 1972.

Fitzgerald, Robert, introduction. *Everything That Rises Must Converge.* By Flannery O'Connor. New York: Farrar, Straus and Giroux, 1965.

Fitzgerald, Sally, editor. *The Habit of Being: The Letters of Flannery O'Connor.* New York: Farrar, Straus, and Giroux, 1979.

Folks, Jeffrey J. "The Mechanical in *Everything That Rises Must Converge.*" *The Southern Literary Journal* 18/2 (Spring 1986): 14-26.

Fowler, Roger. *Linguistics and the Novel.* London: Methuen & Co. Ltd., 1977.

Frank, Marcella. *Modern English: A Practical Reference Guide.* Englewood Cliffs NJ: Prentice-Hall, Inc., 1972.

Friedman, Melvin J. and Lewis A. Lawson. *The Added Dimension: The Art and Mind of Flannery O'Connor.* New York: Fordham University Press, 1966.

Frye, Northrop. *The Great Code: The Bible and Literature.* New York: Harcourt Brace Jovanovich, Publishers, 1982.

Gentry, Marshall Bruce. *Flannery O'Connor's Religion of the Grotesque.* Jackson: University Press of Mississippi, 1986.

Gibson, Walker. "Authors, Speakers, Readers, and Mock Readers." In *Reader-Response Criticism: From Formalism to Post-Structuralism,* edited by Jane P. Tompkins, 1-6. Baltimore: Johns Hopkins University Press, 1980.

Guiraud, Pierre. "Modern Linguistics Looks at Rhetoric: Free Indirect Style." In *Patterns of Literary Style,* edited by Joseph Strelka, 77-89. University Park: Pennsylvania State University Press, 1971.

Hawkes, John. "Flannery O'Connor's Devil." *Sewanee Review* 70/3 (July-September 1962): 9-17. Also, in Harold Bloom, editor. *Flannery O'Connor.* New York: Chelsea House Publishers, 1986.

Charles Herberhann, et al., editors. *The Catholic Encyclopedia: An International Work of Reference on the Constitution, Doctrine, Discipline, and History of the Catholic Church.* 15 volumes. New York: Encyclopedia Press, Inc., 1913.

Hoever, Hugo H., editor. *Saint Joseph Daily Missal.* New York: Catholic Book Publishing Co., 1957.

Jones, Larry Bert. *Pragmatic Aspects of English Text Structure.* Dallas: Summer Institute of Linguistics and The University of Texas at Arlington, 1983.

Kennedy, Chris. "Systemic Grammar and its Use in Literary Analysis." In *Language and Literature: An Introductory Reader in Stylistics,* edited by Ronald Carter, 83-99. London: George Allen & Unwin, 1982.

Kessler, Edward. *Flannery O'Connor and the Language of Apocalypse.* Princeton: Princeton University Press, 1986.

Knapp, Bettina L. *Machine, Metaphor, and the Writer: A Jungian View.* University Park and London: Pennsylvania State University Press, 1989.

Kort, Wesley A. *Narrative Elements and Religious Meaning.* Philadelphia: Fortress Press, 1975.

Lakoff, George and Mark Johnson. *Metaphors We Live By.* Chicago: University of Chicago Press, 1980.

Lawson, Lewis A. "The Perfect Deformity: *Wise Blood.*" *Renascence: Essays on Values in Literature* 17/2 (Spring 1965): 37-41. Also, in Harold Bloom, editor. *Flannery O'Connor.* New York: Chelsea House Publishers, 1986.

Leech, Geoffrey N. and Michael H. Short. *Style in Fiction: A Linguistic Introduction to English Fictional Prose.* London: Longman, 1981.

Maas, A. J. "Salvation." In *The Catholic Encyclopedia*, edited by Charles Herberhann, et al., 13:408. New York: Encyclopedia Press, Inc., 1913.

Maher, Michael, "Free Will." In *The Catholic Encyclopedia*, edited by Charles Herberhann, et al., 6:259-63. New York: Encyclopedia Press, Inc., 1913.

Maio, Eugene A. *St. John of the Cross: The Imagery of Eros.* Madrid: Playor, S. A., 1973.

May, John R. *The Pruning Word: The Parables of Flannery O'Connor.* Notre Dame: University of Notre Dame Press, 1976.

Nida, Eugene A. *Message and Mission: The Communication of the Christian Faith.* New York: Harper & Brothers Publishers, 1960.

O'Connor, Flannery. *Collected Works*, edited by Sally Fitzgerald. New York: Library of America, 1988.

—. *Mystery and Manners: Occasional Prose*, edited by Sally and Robert Fitzgerald. New York: Farrar, Straus and Giroux, 1969.

—. *The Complete Stories.* New York: Farrar, Straus and Giroux, 1971.

Orr, James, ed. *The International Standard Bible Encyclopaedia.* Volume 4. Grand Rapids MI: William B. Eerdmans Publishing Co., 1960.

Orvell, Miles. *Invisible Parade: The Fiction of Flannery O'Connor.* Philadelphia: Temple University Press, 1972.

Parr, Mary. "James Joyce and Catholicism." *Renascence: A Critical Journal of Letters* 13/2 (Winter 1961): 103-106.

Ragen, Brian A. *A Wreck on the Road to Damascus: Innocence, Guilt, & Conversion in Flannery O'Connor.* Chicago: Loyola University Press, 1989.

Ricoeur, Paul. *Time and Narrative.* Volume 3. Chicago: University of Chicago Press, 1985.

Rosenblatt, Louise M. *Literature as Exploration.* New York: Noble and Noble, Publishers, Inc., 1976.

Sheed, F. J. *Theology for Beginners.* Ann Arbor MI: Servant Books, 1981.

Shloss, Carol. *Flannery O'Connor's Dark Comedies: The Limits of Inference.* Baton Rouge: Louisiana State University Press, 1980.

Silva, Marilyn N. *Grammar in Many Voices.* Lincolnwood IL: NTC Publishing Group, 1995.

Stephens, Martha. *The Question of Flannery O'Connor.* Baton Rouge: Louisiana State University Press, 1973.

Traugott, Elizabeth Closs and Mary Louise Pratt. *Linguistics for Students of Literature.* New York: Harcourt Brace Jovanovich, Inc. 1980.

Index

ALBERTSON COLLEGE OF IDAHO
3 5556 0013 7247 3